1/4

· A ·
GOOD·BOOK
· IS · THE ·
PRECIOUS
LIFE–BLOOD
· OF · A ·
MASTER
SPIRIT
Milton

PRINTED IN GREAT BRITAIN

D1437327

The KING'S TREASURIES
OF LITERATURE

GENERAL EDITOR
SIR A·T· QUILLER COUCH

NEW·YORK·E·P·DUTTON·AND·CO·IN·

CARLYLE

NEW·YORK · E·P·DUTTON ·AND·CO·IN

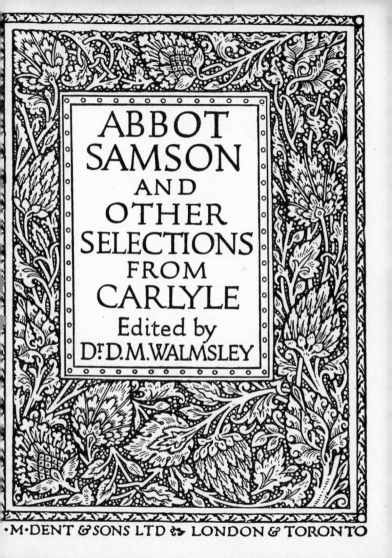

ABBOT SAMSON AND OTHER SELECTIONS FROM CARLYLE

Edited by
Dr D.M.WALMSLEY

·M·DENT & SONS LTD ॐ LONDON & TORONTO

All rights reserved

First Published in this Edition . 1934

PRINTED IN GREAT BRITAIN

INTRODUCTION

MANY readers may have been prejudiced against Carlyle as a result of a premature attempt to read through a difficult work like *Sartor Resartus,* or the weighty volumes of the *French Revolution.* Of the bulk of his work a large proportion is unlikely to be read save by a few students. Much may indeed be omitted without serious loss, for Carlyle is a prolix writer, over-fond of repeating favourite ideas and beliefs. In the present selection the passages chosen show Carlyle at his best as a narrative and descriptive writer; his more abstruse and controversial works are not represented. *Abbot Samson,* the first and longest of the pieces, affords perhaps the most attractive introduction to Carlyle, whilst the portraits and historical episodes that follow illustrate the range and variety of his work, his powers of depicting scenes and characters in vigorous prose, always expressive of a strong personality with deep convictions tempered by a keen sense of humour.

The story of Abbot Samson is taken from Book II of *Past and Present,* published in 1843. As the title suggests, the writer's purpose is to compare and contrast the conditions of life in an earlier period of our history with those of his own day. What led to the choice of a medieval monastery as an illustration was the reading of a detailed first-hand account written by a monk named Jocelyn of Brakelond in the twelfth century and printed by the Camden Society in 1840. Jocelyn's chronicle is written in Latin, the universal language of scholars in the Middle Ages. He began

writing it in the year 1173, when he had completed his
novitiate under Samson, who at that time was master
of the novices.   Later, Jocelyn became prior's chaplain,
and soon after Samson's election he was appointed
abbot's chaplain.   At the time of Abbot Samson's death,
he was serving in the office of almoner.

In his first chapter Carlyle asserts with emphasis the
superiority of the 'poorest historical Fact' over 'all
Fiction whatsoever', and he implies that his story is a
literal rendering of a narrative that was actually true
in every detail.   This suggestion is further strengthened
by his practice of inserting now and then words and
phrases from the original Latin.   It is to be borne in
mind, however, that his purpose was to present a picture
of an ideal way of life.   His version is in fact something
more than even a free translation: it is an imaginative
reconstruction of the original that bears on every page
the impress of Carlyle's own personality.   He has, consciously or unconsciously, taken in some measure the
liberties of the novelist, or at any rate of the artist, who
selects and modifies his material to suit his purpose.
Hence, while most of the concrete facts given about the
monastery and its work may be accepted as true, the
reader must make due allowance for certain significant
omissions and be careful to distinguish between the
facts and Carlyle's interpretation of the facts.   Further,
Jocelyn himself like most early writers was uncritical,
and would naturally stress the pleasanter side of the
community of which he was a member, bound by his
vows to set an example of piety and obedience.   Yet
even he did not always approve of the abbot's ways,
and he records incidents, of which Carlyle says nothing,
that go to show that the monks regarded their superior
as something of a tyrant.   When all allowances have

been made, however, the picture of monastic life presented is far more faithful and complete than those that may be found in popular fiction, while the portrait of Samson has its own value as an interpretation of human character.

The abbey over which Samson ruled was a Benedictine monastery founded by Canute in 1028 at Beodricsworth, afterwards called Bury (i.e. 'Borough') St. Edmunds, where the remains of the saint, a king of East Anglia martyred by the Danes about the year 870, were enshrined. Before Samson became abbot in 1182 the monastery had been greatly enlarged, and with increasing wealth and independence of control it had become worldly and corrupt, burdened with debts and feebly governed. Abbot Samson restored its prosperity. For thirty years he ruled, wisely and firmly, enriching it, says the chronicler, 'with privileges, liberties, possessions, and spacious buildings, and restored the worship of the Church both internally and externally in the most ample manner'. St. Edmund's was indeed one of the largest abbeys in the country. Little idea of its extent and widespread influence can be obtained from a view of the ruins still standing. The monastic buildings lay to the north side of the great cruciform church more than five hundred feet in length. Within the precincts were employed about two hundred and fifty men, including eighty monks and fifty priests and chaplains. There were also numerous farms and mills directly dependent on the abbey. The abbot, venerated as the representative of Christ, ruled with almost absolute power. He appointed all the officials of the monastery, including the prior, who was responsible for discipline and acted as the abbot's deputy, the sub-prior his assistant, and the subordinate officials known as

obedientiaries. The daily routine began at midnight
with the chanting of prayers in the choir, lasting about an
hour, after which the monks retired to bed until 6 a.m.
Services and a meeting of the Chapter to discuss business and discipline took up the morning until 11 a.m.,
when dinner was served. After an hour's rest and
further prayers some worked in the fields or on the
buildings, others employed their time in their cells on
manuscripts or other indoor crafts. Supper was served
at 5 p.m. in winter, and 6 p.m. in summer, the final
service being held two hours later. The routine varied
slightly in different monasteries and at different periods.

Carlyle frequently interrupts the course of the narrative in order to bring out the contrast between the ideal
life of the monastery with degenerate conditions he saw
around him: lack of true religion, neglect of the things
of the mind, all the evils attributed to industrialism
with its worship of Mammon. A few of the longer
comments have been omitted in the present text. The
abbot himself is exalted as an example of a true 'Hero',
whose function is, in Carlyle's view, to govern and
regulate the affairs of men in accordance with the
divine will. In essential qualities, therefore, he may
be compared with the more famous characters represented in this book. All illustrate in various ways
Carlyle's doctrine of the Hero, of which more will be
said in the Commentary.

CONTENTS

HISTORICAL EPISODES

ABBOT SAMSON

ABBOT SAMSON

ABBOT SAMSON

CHAPTER I

JOCELIN OF BRAKELOND

A CERTAIN Jocelinus de Brakelonda, a natural-born Englishman, has left us an extremely foreign Book, which the labours of the Camden Society have brought to light in these days. Jocelin's Book, the 'Chronicle', or private Boswellean Notebook, of Jocelin, a certain old St. Edmundsbury Monk and Boswell, now seven centuries old, how remote is it from us; exotic, extraneous; in all ways, coming from far abroad! The language of it is not foreign only but dead: Monk-Latin lies across not the British Channel, but the ninefold Stygian Marshes, Stream of Lethe, and one knows not where! Roman Latin itself, still alive for us in the Elysian Fields of Memory, is domestic in comparison. And then the ideas, life-furniture, whole workings and ways of this worthy Jocelin; covered deeper than Pompeii with the lava-ashes and inarticulate wreck of seven hundred years!

Jocelin of Brakelond cannot be called a conspicuous literary character; indeed few mortals that have left so visible a work, or footmark, behind them can be more

Camden Society. Named after the Elizabethan antiquary, William Camden; founded for the purpose of studying and publishing medieval and other texts.

obscure.   One other of those vanished Existences, whose
work has not yet vanished—almost a pathetic phenomenon, were not the whole world full of such!   The
builders of Stonehenge, for example—or, alas, what
say we, Stonehenge and builders?   The writers of the
Universal Review and *Homer's Iliad*; the paviors of
London streets—sooner or later, the entire Posterity
of Adam!   It is a pathetic phenomenon; but an
irremediable, nay, if well meditated, a consoling one.

By his dialect of Monk-Latin, and indeed by his
name, this Jocelin seems to have been a Norman
Englishman; the surname *de Brakelonda* indicates a
native of St. Edmundsbury itself, *Brakelond* being the
known old name of a street or quarter in that venerable
Town.   Then farther, sure enough, our Jocelin was a
Monk   of   St.   Edmundsbury   Convent;   held   some
'*obedientia*', subaltern officiality there, or rather, in
succession several; was, for one thing, 'chaplain to my
Lord Abbot, living beside him night and day for the
space of six years'—which last, indeed, is the grand
fact of Jocelin's existence, and properly the origin of
this present Book, and of the chief meaning it has for
us now.   He was, as we have hinted, a kind of born
Boswell, though an infinitesimally small one; neither did
he altogether want his *Johnson* even there and then.
Johnsons are rare; yet, as has been asserted, Boswells
perhaps still rarer—the more is the pity on both sides!
This Jocelin, as we can discern well, was an ingenious

Universal Review. A short-lived monthly magazine, published
in 1824–5.
Obedientia. The office of an obedientiary, a minor official of
a monastery.

and ingenuous, a cheery-hearted, innocent, yet withal shrewd, noticing, quick-witted man; and from under his monk's cowl has looked out on that narrow section of the world in a really *human* manner; not in any *simial*, canine, ovine, or otherwise *in*human manner—afflictive to all that have humanity! The man is of patient, peaceable, loving, clear-smiling nature; open for this and that. A wise simplicity is in him; much natural sense; a *veracity* that goes deeper than words. Veracity: it is the basis of all; and, some say, means genius itself; the prime essence of all genius whatsoever. Our Jocelin, for the rest, has read his classical manuscripts, his Virgilius, his Flaccus, Ovidius Naso; of course still more, his Homilies and Breviaries, and if not the Bible, considerable extracts of the Bible. Then also he has a pleasant wit; and loves a timely joke, though in mild subdued manner; very amiable to see. A learned grown man, yet with the heart as of a good child; whose whole life indeed has been that of a child—St. Edmundsbury Monastery a larger kind of cradle for him in which his whole prescribed duty was to *sleep* kindly, and love his mother well! This is the Biography of Jocelin; 'a man of excellent religion', says one of his contemporary Brother Monks, '*eximiæ religionis, potens sermone et opere*'.

We have heard so much of Monks; everywhere, in real and fictitious History, from Muratori Annals to

Simial. Ape-like.

Eximiæ, etc. 'Of excellent religion, strong in word and deed.'

Muratori Annals. A collection, in 28 folio volumes, of sources of Italian history; compiled by L. A. Muratori in the eighteenth century.

Radcliffe Romances, these singular two-legged animals,
with their rosaries and breviaries, with their shaven
crowns, hair-cilices, and vows of poverty, masquerade
so strangely through our fancy; and they are in fact so
very strange an extinct species of the human family—
a veritable Monk of Bury St. Edmunds is worth attend-
ing to, if by chance made visible and audible. Here he
is; and in his hand a magical speculum, much gone to
rust indeed, yet in fragments still clear; wherein the
marvellous image of his existence does still shadow
itself, though fitfully, and as with an intermittent light!
Will not the reader peep with us into this singular
camera lucida, where an extinct species, though fitfully,
can still be seen alive? Extinct species, we say; for the
live specimens which still go about under that character
are too evidently to be classed as spurious in Natural
History: the Gospel of Richard Arkwright once pro-
mulgated, no Monk of the old sort is any longer possible
in this world. But fancy a deep-buried Mastodon, some
fossil Megatherion, Ichthyosaurus, were to begin to
speak from amid its rock-swathings, never so indis-
tinctly! The most extinct fossil species of Men or
Monks can do, and does, this miracle—thanks to the
Letters of the Alphabet, good for so many things.

Jocelin, we said, was somewhat of a Boswell; but

Hair-cilices. Rough garments of hair-cloth.

Radcliffe Romances. Anne Radcliffe, 1764–1823, was a
popular writer of romantic stories with medieval settings.

Camera lucida. An apparatus for projecting pictures of
distant objects upon paper, by means of a glass prism.

Gospel of Richard Arkwright. Industrialism, initiated by
Arkwright's invention of the spinning frame, 1771, and similar
machines.

unfortunately, by Nature, he is none of the largest, and distance has now dwarfed him to an extreme degree. His light is most feeble, intermittent, and requires the intensest kindest inspection; otherwise, it will disclose mere vacant haze. It must be owned, the good Jocelin, spite of his beautiful child-like character, is but an altogether imperfect 'mirror' of these old-world things! The good man, he looks on us so clear and cheery, and in his neighbourly soft-smiling eyes we see so well our *own* shadow—we have a longing always to cross-question him, to force from him an explanation of much. But no; Jocelin, though he talks with such clear familiarity, like a next-door neighbour, will not answer any question: that is the peculiarity of him, dead these six hundred and fifty years, and quite deaf to us, though still so audible! The good man, he cannot help it, nor can we.

But truly it is a strange consideration this simple one, as we go on with him, or indeed with any lucid simple-hearted soul like him: Behold therefore, this England of the Year 1200 was no chimerical vacuity or dreamland, peopled with mere vaporous Fantasms, Rymer's Fœdera, and Doctrines of the Constitution; but a green solid place, that grew corn and several other things. The Sun shone on it; the vicissitude of seasons and human fortunes. Cloth was woven and worn; ditches were dug, furrow-fields ploughed, and houses built. Day by day all men and cattle rose to

Rymer's Fœdera. A monumental collection of treaties, etc., dating from the Norman Conquest, made by Thomas Rymer (died 1713).

labour, and night by night returned home weary to
their several lairs. In wondrous Dualism, then as now,
lived nations of breathing men; alternating, in all ways,
between Light and Dark; between joy and sorrow,
between rest and toil—between hope, hope reaching
high as Heaven, and fear deep as very Hell. Not
vapour Fantasms, Rymer's Fœdera at all! Cœur-de-
Lion was not a theatrical popinjay with greaves and
steel-cap on it, but a man living upon victuals—*not*
imported by Peel's Tariff. Cœur-de-Lion came palpably
athwart this Jocelin at St. Edmundsbury; and had
almost peeled the sacred gold '*Feretrum*', or St. Edmund
Shrine itself, to ransom him out of the Danube Jail.

These clear eyes of neighbour Jocelin looked on the
bodily presence of King John; the very John *Sansterre*,
or Lackland, who signed *Magna Charta* afterwards in
Runnymead. Lackland, with a great retinue, boarded
once, for the matter of a fortnight, in St. Edmundsbury
Convent; daily in the very eyesight, palpable to the very
fingers of our Jocelin: O Jocelin, what did he say, what
did he do; how looked he, lived he—at the very lowest,
what coat or breeches had he on? Jocelin is obstinately
silent. Jocelin marks down what interests *him*; entirely
deaf to *us*. With Jocelin's eyes we discern almost
nothing of John Lackland. As through a glass darkly,
we with our own eyes and appliances, intensely looking,
discern at most: A blustering, dissipated human figure,
with a kind of blackguard quality air, in cramoisy
velvet, or other uncertain texture, uncertain cut, with
much plumage and fringing; amid numerous other

Cramoisy. Crimson.

human figures of the like; riding abroad with hawks;
talking noisy nonsense;—tearing out the bowels of
St. Edmundsbury Convent (its larders namely and
cellars) in the most ruinous way, by living at rack and
manger there. Jocelin notes only, with a slight sub-
acidity of manner, that the King's Majesty, *Dominus
Rex*, did leave, as gift for our St. Edmund Shrine, a
handsome enough silk cloak—or rather pretended to
leave, for one of his retinue borrowed it of us, and *we*
never got sight of it again; and, on the whole, that the
Dominus Rex, at departing, gave us 'thirteen *sterlingii*',
one shilling and one penny, to say a mass for him; and
so departed—like a shabby Lackland as he was!
'Thirteen pence sterling', this was what the Convent
got from Lackland, for all the victuals he and his had
made away with. We of course said our mass for him,
having covenanted to do it—but let impartial posterity
judge with what degree of fervour!

And in this manner vanishes King Lackland; traverses
swiftly our strange intermittent magic-mirror, jingling
the shabby thirteen pence merely; and rides with his
hawks into Egyptian night again. It is Jocelin's manner
with all things; and it is men's manner and men's
necessity. How intermittent is our good Jocelin;
marking down, without eye to *us*, what *he* finds interesting! How much in Jocelin, as in all History,
and indeed in all Nature, is at once inscrutable and
certain; so dim, yet so indubitable; exciting us to
endless considerations. For King Lackland *was* there,
verily he; and did leave these *tredecim sterlingii*, if
nothing more, and did live and look in one way or the

other, and a whole world was living and looking along with him! There, we say, is the grand peculiarity; the immeasurable one; distinguishing, to a really infinite degree, the poorest historical Fact from all Fiction whatsoever. Fiction, 'Imagination', 'Imaginative Poetry', etc. etc., except as the vehicle for truth, or *fact* of some sort—which surely a man should first try various other ways of vehiculating, and conveying safe —what is it? Let the Minerva and other Presses respond!

But it is time we were in St. Edmundsbury Monastery and Seven good Centuries off. If indeed it be possible, by any aid of Jocelin, by any human art, to get thither, with a reader or two still following us?

Minerva Press. Publishers of cheap fiction, early nineteenth century.

CHAPTER II

ST. EDMUNDSBURY

THE *Burg*, Bury, or 'Berry' as they call it, of St. Edmund
is still a prosperous brisk Town; beautifully diversifying,
with its clear brick houses, ancient clean streets, and
twenty or fifteen thousand busy souls, the general grassy
face of Suffolk; looking out right pleasantly, from its
hill-slope, towards the rising Sun: and on the eastern
edge of it, still runs, long, black, and massive, a range
of monastic ruins; into the wide internal spaces of which
the stranger is admitted on payment of one shilling.
Internal spaces laid out, at present, as a botanic garden.
Here stranger or townsman, sauntering at his leisure
amid these vast grim venerable ruins, may persuade
himself that an Abbey of St. Edmundsbury did once
exist; nay there is no doubt of it: see here the ancient
massive Gateway, of architecture interesting to the eye
of Dilettantism; and farther on, that other ancient
Gateway, now about to tumble, unless Dilettantism, in
these very months, can subscribe money to cramp it
and prop it!

Here, sure enough, is an Abbey; beautiful in the eye
of Dilettantism. Giant Pedantry also will step in, with
its huge *Dugdale* and other enormous *Monasticons* under

Dilettantism. Used here, by metonymy, for *dilettanti*, superficial lovers of the arts.

Dugdale. Seventeenth-century author of *Monasticon Angli-
canum*, a compendious history of monasteries.

its arm, and cheerfully apprise you, That this was a
very great Abbey, owner and indeed creator of St.
Edmund's Town itself, owner of wide lands and revenues;
nay that its land were once a county of themselves; that
indeed King Canute or Knut was very kind to it, and
gave St. Edmund his own gold crown off his head, on
one occasion: for the rest, that the Monks were of such
and such a genus, such and such a number; that they
had so many carucates of land in this hundred, and so
many in that; and then farther that the large Tower or
Belfry was built by such a one, and the smaller Belfry
was built by etc. etc.—Till human nature can stand no
more of it; till human nature desperately take refuge
in forgetfulness, almost in flat disbelief of the whole
business, Monks, Monastery, Belfries, Carucates and all!
Alas, what mountains of dead ashes, wreck, and burnt
bones, does assiduous Pedantry dig up from the Past
Time, and name it History, and Philosophy of History;
till, as we say, the human soul sinks wearied and bewil-
dered; till the Past Time seems all one infinite incredible
gray void, without sun, stars, hearth-fires, or candle-
light; dim offensive dust-whirlwinds filling universal
Nature; and over your Historical Library, it is as if all
the Titans had written for themselves: Dry Rubbish
shot here!

And yet these grim old walls are not a dilettantism
and dubiety; they are an earnest fact. It was a most
real and serious purpose they were built for! Yes,
another world it was, when these black ruins, white in

    Carucate. An area of land that could be ploughed in a year
by a team of eight oxen (Lat. *carruca,* a plough).

their new mortar and fresh chiselling, first saw the sun as walls, long ago. Gauge not, with thy dilettante compasses, with that placid dilettante simper, the Heaven's-Watchtower of our Fathers, the fallen God's-Houses, the Golgotha of true Souls departed!

Their architecture, belfries, land-carucates? Yes— and that is but a small item of the matter. Does it never give thee pause, this other strange item of it, that men then had a *soul*—not by hearsay alone, and as a figure of speech; but as a truth that they *knew*, and practically went upon! Verily it was another world then. Their Missals have become incredible, a sheer platitude, sayest thou? Yes, a most poor platitude; and even, if thou wilt, an idolatory and blasphemy, should any one persuade *thee* to believe them, to pretend praying by them.

Another world, truly: and this present poor distressed world might get some profit by looking wisely into it, instead of foolishly. But at lowest, O dilettante friend, let us know always that it *was* a world, and not a void infinite of gray haze with fantasms swimming in it. These old St. Edmundsbury walls, I say, were not people with fantasms; but with men of flesh and blood, made altogether as we are. Had thou and I then been, who knows but we ourselves had taken refuge from an evil Time, and fled to dwell here, and meditate on an Eternity, in such fashion as we could? Alas, how like an old osseous fragment, a broken blackened shin-bone of the old dead Ages, this black ruin looks out, not yet covered by the soil; still indicating what a once gigantic Life lies buried there! It is dead now, and dumb; but was alive once, and spake. For twenty generations, here was the earthly arena where painful living men worked out their life-wrestle—looked at by Earth, by Heaven and Hell. Bells tolled to prayers; and men, of many humours, various thoughts, chanted vespers, matins; and round the little islet of their life rolled forever (as round ours still rolls, though we are blind and deaf) the illimitable Ocean, tinting all things with *its* eternal hues and reflexes; making strange prophetic music! How silent now; all departed, clean gone. The World-Dramaturgist has written: *Exeunt*. The devouring Time-Demons have made away with it all: and in its stead, there is either nothing; or what is worse, offensive universal dust-clouds, and grey eclipse of Earth and Heaven, from 'dry rubbish shot here'!

Truly it is no easy matter to get across the chasm of Seven Centuries, filled with such material. But here, of all helps, is not a Boswell the welcomest; even a small Boswell? Veracity, true simplicity of heart, how valuable are these always! He that speaks what *is* really in him, will find men to listen, though under never such impediments. Even gossip, springing free and cheery from a human heart, this too is a kind of veracity and *speech*—much preferable to pedantry and inane grey haze! Jocelin is weak and garrulous, but he is human. Through the thin watery gossip of our Jocelin, we do get some glimpses of that deep-buried Time; discern veritably, though in a fitful intermittent manner, these antique figures and their life-method, face to face! Beautifully, in our earnest loving glance, the old centuries melt from opaque to partially translucent, transparent here and there; and the void black Night, one finds, is but the summing-up of innumerable peopled luminous *Days*. Not parchment Chartularies, Doctrines of the Constitution, O Dryasdust; not altogether, my erudite friend!

Readers who please to go along with us into this poor *Jocelini Chronica* shall wander inconveniently enough, as in wintry twilight, through some poor stript hazel-grove, rustling with foolish noises, and perpetually hindering the eyesight; but across which, here and there, some real human figure is seen moving: very strange; whom we could hail if he would answer—and we look into a pair of eyes deep as our own, *imaging* our own, but all unconscious of us; to whom we, for the time, are become as spirits and invisible!

Chartularies. Medieval records, especially of monasteries.

CHAPTER III

LANDLORD EDMUND

SOME three centuries or so had elapsed since *Beodric's-worth* became St. Edmund's *Stow*, St. Edmund's *Town* and Monastery, before Jocelin entered himself a Novice there. 'It was', says he, 'the year after the Flemings were defeated at Fornham St. Genevieve.'

Much passes away into oblivion: this glorious victory over the Flemings at Fornham has, at the present date, greatly dimmed itself out of the minds of men. A victory and battle nevertheless it was, in its time: some thrice-renowned Earl of Leicester, not of the De Montfort breed (as may be read in Philosophical and other Histories, could any human memory retain such things), had quarrelled with his sovereign, Henry Second of the name; had been worsted, it is like, and maltreated, and obliged to fly to foreign parts; but had rallied there into new vigour; and so, in the year 1173, returns across the German Sea with a vengeful army of Flemings. Returns, to the coast of Suffolk; to Framlingham Castle, where he is welcomed; westward towards St. Edmunds-bury and Fornham Church, where he is met by the constituted authorities with *posse comitatus*; and swiftly cut in pieces, he and his, or laid by the heels; on the

Fornham St. Genevieve. Four miles north of Bury St. Edmunds.

right bank of the obscure river Lark—as traces still existing will verify.

For the river Lark, though not very discoverably, still runs or stagnates in that country; and the battle-ground is there; serving at present as a pleasure-ground to his Grace of Northumberland. Copper pennies of Henry II are still found there—rotted out from the pouches of poor slain soldiers, who had not had *time* to buy liquor with them. In the river Lark itself was fished up, within man's memory, an antique gold ring; which fond Dilettantism can almost believe may have been the very ring Countess Leicester threw away, in her flight, into that same Lark river or ditch. Nay, few years ago, in tearing out an enormous superannuated ash-tree, now grown quite corpulent, bursten, super-fluous, but long a fixture in the soil, and not to be dislodged without revolution—there was laid bare, under its roots, 'a circular mound of skeletons wonderfully complete', all radiating from a centre, faces upwards, feet inwards; a 'radiation' not of Light, but of the Nether Darkness rather; and evidently the fruit of battle; for 'many of the heads were cleft, or had arrow-holes in them'. The Battle of Fornham, therefore, is a fact, though a forgotten one; no less obscure than undeniable —like so many other facts.

Like the St. Edmund's Monastery itself! Who can doubt, after what we have said, that there was a Monas-tery here at one time? No doubt at all there was a Monastery here; no doubt, some three centuries prior to this Fornham Battle, there dwelt a man in these parts of the name of Edmund, King, Landlord, Duke, or whatever his title was, of the Eastern Counties—and a very singular man and landlord he must have been.

For his tenants, it would appear, did not in the least complain of him; his labourers did not think of burning his wheat stacks, breaking into his game-preserves; very far the reverse of all that. Clear evidence, satisfactory even to my friend Dryasdust, exists that, on the contrary, they honoured, loved, admired this ancient Landlord to a quite astonishing degree—and indeed at last to an immeasurable and inexpressible degree; for, finding no limits or utterable words for their sense of his worth, they took to beatifying and adoring him! 'Infinite admiration', we are taught, 'means worship'.

Very singular—could we discover it! What Edmund's specific duties were; above all, what his method of discharging them with such results was, would surely be interesting to know; but are *not* very discoverable now. His life has become a poetic, nay a religious *Mythus*; though, undeniably enough, it was once a prose Fact, as our poor lives are; and even a very rugged unmanageable one. This landlord Edmund did go about in leather shoes, with *femoralia* and bodycoat of some sort on him; and daily had his breakfast to procure; and daily had contradictory speeches, and most contradictory facts not a few, to reconcile with himself. No man becomes a Saint in his sleep. Edmund, for instance, instead of *reconciling* those same contradictory facts and speeches to himself—which means *subduing*, and in a manlike and godlike manner conquering them

Femoralia. Breeches.

to himself—might have merely thrown new contention into them, new unwisdom into them, and so been conquered *by* them; much the commoner case! In that way he had proved no 'Saint', or Divine-looking Man, but a mere Sinner, and unfortunate, blameable, more or less Diabolic-looking man! No landlord Edmund becomes infinitely admirable in his sleep.

With what degree of wholesome rigour his rents were collected, we hear not. Still less by what methods he preserved his game, whether by 'bushing' or how—and if the partridge-seasons were 'excellent', or were indifferent. Neither do we ascertain what kind of Corn-bill he passed, or wisely-adjusted Sliding-scale—but indeed there were few spinners in those days; and the nuisance of spinning, and other dusty labour, was not yet so glaring a one.

How then, it may be asked, did this Edmund rise into favour; become to such astonishing extent a recognized Farmer's Friend? Really, except it were by doing justly and loving mercy to an unprecedented extent, one does not know. The man, it would seem 'had walked', as they say, 'humbly with God'; humbly and valiantly with God; struggling to make the Earth heavenly as he could: instead of walking sumptuously and pridefully with Mammon, leaving the Earth to grow hellish as it liked. Not sumptuously with Mammon? How then could he 'encourage trade'—cause Howel and James, and many wine-merchants, to bless him, and the tailor's heart (though in a very short-sighted manner) to sing for joy? Much in this Edmund's Life is mysterious.

That he could, on occasion, do what he liked with his own, is meanwhile evident enough. Certain Heathen Physical-Force Ultra-Chartists, 'Danes' as they were then called, coming into his territory with their 'five points', or rather with their five-and-twenty thousand *points* and edges too, of pikes namely and battle-axes; and proposing mere Heathenism, confiscation, spoliation, and fire and sword—Edmund answered that he would oppose to the utmost such savagery. They took him prisoner; again required his sanction to said proposals. Edmund again refused. Cannot we kill you? cried they. —Cannot I die? answered he. My life, I think, is my own to do what I like with! And he died, under barbarous tortures, refusing to the last breath; and the Ultra-Chartist Danes *lost* their propositions—and went with their 'points' and other apparatus, as is supposed, to the Devil, the Father of them. Some say, indeed, these Danes were not Ultra-Chartists, but Ultra-Tories, demanding to reap where they had not sown, and live in this world without working, though all the world should starve for it; which likewise seems a possible hypothesis. Be what they might, they went, as we say, to the Devil; and Edmund doing what he liked with his own, the Earth was got cleared of them.

Another version is, that Edmund on this and the like occasions stood by his order; the oldest, and indeed only true order of Nobility known under the stars, that of Just Men and Sons of God, in opposition to Unjust

Physical-Force Ultra-Chartists. Carlyle makes a rather forced comparison between the demands of the Danes and the five points or articles of the People's Charter of 1838. There were Physical Force Chartists and Moral Force Chartists.

and Sons of Belial—which latter indeed are *second*-oldest, but yet a very unvenerable order. This, truly, seems the likeliest hypothesis of all. Names and appearances alter so strangely, in some half-score centuries; and all fluctuates chameleon-like, taking now this hue, now that. Thus much is very plain, and does not change hue; Landlord Edmund was seen and felt by all men to have done verily a man's part in this life-pilgrimage of his; and benedictions, and outflowing love and admiration from the universal heart, were his meed. Well done! Well done! cried the hearts of all men. They raised his slain and martyred body; washed its wounds with fast-flowing universal tears; tears of endless pity, and yet of a sacred joy and triumph. The beautifulest kind of tears—indeed perhaps the beautifulest kind of thing: like a sky all flashing diamonds and prismatic radiance; all weeping, yet shone on by the everlasting Sun—and *this* is not a sky, it is a Soul and living Face! Nothing liker the *Temple of the Highest*, bright with some real effulgence of the Highest, is seen in this world.

Oh, if all Yankee-land follow a small good 'Schnüspel the distinguished Novelist' with blazing torches, dinner-invitations, universal hep-hep-hurrah, feeling that he, though small, *is* something; how might all Angle-land once follow a hero-martyr and great true Son of Heaven! It is the very joy of man's heart to admire, where he can; nothing so lifts h m from all his mean imprison-

---

Schnüspel. A name probably invented by Carlyle as a type of popular novelist; actually refers to Charles Dickens, to whom Carlyle afterwards made amends for this contemptuous reference.

ments, were it but for moments, as true admiration.
Thus it has been said, 'all men, especially all women,
are born worshippers'; and will worship, if it be but
possible.   Possible to worship a Something, even a small
one; not so possible a mere loud-blaring Nothing! What
sight is more pathetic than that of poor multitudes of
persons met to gaze at Kings' Progresses, Lord Mayors'
Shows, and other gilt-gingerbread phenomena of the
worshipful sort, in these times; each so eager to worship;
each, with a dim fatal sense of disappointment, finding
that he cannot rightly here!   These be thy gods, O Israel?
And thou art so *willing* to worship—poor Israel!

In this manner, however, did the men of the Eastern
Counties take up the slain body of their Edmund, where
it lay cast forth in the village of Hoxne; seek out the
severed head, and reverently reunite the same.   They
embalmed him with myrrh and sweet spices, with love,
pity, and all high and awful thoughts; consecrating him
with a very storm of melodious adoring admiration, and
sun-dyed showers of tears—joyfully, yet with awe (as
all deep joy has something of the awful in it), com-
memorating his noble deeds and godlike walk and conversation while on Earth.   Till, at length, the very Pope
and Cardinals at Rome were forced to hear of it; and
they, summing up as correctly as they well could, with
Advocatus-Diaboli pleadings and their other forms of
process, the general verdict of mankind, declared: That
he had, in very fact, led a hero's life in this world; and

Advocatus Diaboli. The Devil's Advocate, who pleaded
against *Advocatus Dei* in the examination at Rome for the
canonization of a saint.

being now *gone*, was gone, as they conceived, to God above, and reaping his reward *there*. Such, they said, was the best judgment they could form of the case—and truly not a bad judgment. Acquiesced in, zealously adopted, with full assent of 'private judgment', by all mortals.

The rest of St. Edmund's history, for the reader sees he has now become a *Saint*, is easily conceivable. Pious munificence provided him a *loculus*, a *feretrum* or shrine; built for him a wooden chapel, a stone temple, ever widening and growing by new pious gifts—such the overflowing heart feels it a blessedness to solace itself by giving. St. Edmund's Shrine glitters now with diamond flowerages, with a plating of wrought gold. The wooden chapel, as we say, has become a stone temple. Stately masonries, long-drawn arches, cloisters, sounding aisles buttress it, begirdle it far and wide. Regimented companies of men, of whom our Jocelin is one, devote themselves, in every generation, to meditate here on man's Nobleness and Awfulness, and celebrate and show forth the same, as they best can—thinking they will do it better here, in presence of God the Maker, and of the so Awful and so Noble made by Him. In one word, St. Edmund's Body has raised a Monastery round it. To such length, in such manner, has the Spirit of the Time visibly taken body, and crystallized itself here. New gifts, houses, farms, *katalla*—come ever in. King Knut, whom men call Canute, whom the

Katalla. Low Latin, *catalla*, cattle; but Carlyle in a note takes it in the sense of *chattels*, a word of the same origin.

B

Oceantide would not be forbidden to wet—we heard already of this wise King, with his crown and gifts; but of many others, Kings, Queens, wise men and noble loyal women, let Dryasdust and divine Silence be the record! Beodric's-Worth has become St. Edmund's *Bury*—and lasts visible to this hour. All this that thou now seest, and namest Bury Town, is properly the Funeral Monument of Saint or Landlord Edmund. The present respectable Mayor of Bury may be said, like a Fakeer (little as he thinks of it), to have his dwelling in the extensive, many-sculptured Tombstone of St. Edmund; in one of the brick niches thereof dwells the present respectable Mayor of Bury.

Certain Times do crystallize themselves in a magnificent manner; and others, perhaps, are like to do it in rather a shabby one! But Richard Arkwright too will have his Monument, a thousand years hence: all Lancashire and Yorkshire, and how many other shires and countries, with their machineries and industries, for his monument! A true *pyr*amid or '*flame*-mountain', flaming with steam fires and useful labour over wide continents, usefully towards the Stars, to a certain height—how much grander than your foolish Cheops Pyramids or Sakhara clay ones! Let us withal be hopeful, be content or patient.

Pyramid. The derivation from Greek *pyr*, fire, is probably incorrect, the word more likely being of Egyptian origin.

CHAPTER IV

ABBOT HUGO

It is true all things have two faces, a light one and
a dark. It is true, in three centuries much imperfec-
tion accumulates; many an Ideal, monastic or other,
shooting forth into practice as it can, grows to a strange
enough Reality; and we have to ask with amazement,
Is this your Ideal! For, alas, the Ideal always has to
grow in the Real, and to seek out its bed and board
there, often in a very sorry way. No beautifulest Poet
is a Bird-of-Paradise, living on perfumes; sleeping in
the ether with outspread wings. The Heroic, *indepen-
dent* of bed and board, is found in Drury Lane Theatre
only; to avoid disappointments, let us bear this in mind.

By the law of Nature, too, all manner of Ideals have
their fatal limits and lot; their appointed periods, of
youth, of maturity or perfection, of decline, degradation,
and final death and disappearance. There is nothing
born but has to die. Ideal monasteries, once grown real,
do seek bed and board in this world; do find it more
and more successfully; do get at length too intent on
finding it, exclusively intent on that. They are then
like diseased corpulent bodies fallen idiotic, which
merely eat and sleep; *ready* for 'dissolution', by a Henry
the Eighth or some other. Jocelin's St. Edmundsbury
is still far from this last dreadful state; but here too the

reader will prepare himself to see an Ideal not sleeping
in the ether like a bird-of-paradise, but roosting as the
common wood-fowl do, in an imperfect, uncomfortable,
more or less contemptible manner!

Abbot Hugo, as Jocelin, breaking at once into the
heart of the business, apprises us, had in those days
grown old, grown rather blind, and his eyes were somewhat darkened, *aliquantulum caligaverunt oculi ejus.*
He dwelt apart very much, in his *Talamus* or peculiar
Chamber; got into the hands of flatterers, a set of mealy-
mouthed persons who strove to make the passing hour
easy for him—for him easy, and for themselves profitable; accumulating in the distance mere mountains of
confusion. Old Dominus Hugo sat inaccessible in this
way, far in the interior, wrapt in his warm flannels and
delusions; inaccessible to all voice of Fact; and bad
grew ever worse with us. Not that our worthy old
Dominus Abbas was inattentive to the divine offices, or
to the maintenance of a devout spirit in us or in himself; but the Account-Books of the Convent fell into
the frightfulest state, and Hugo's annual Budget grew
yearly emptier, or filled with futile expectations, fatal
deficit, wind, and debts!

His one worldly care was to raise ready money;
sufficient for the day is the evil thereof. And how he
raised it: From usurious insatiable Jews; every fresh
Jew sticking on him like a fresh horseleech, sucking his
and our life out; crying continually, Give, give! Take
one example instead of scores. Our *Camera* having

Camera. Here seems to mean *treasury.*

fallen into ruin, William the Sacristan received charge
to repair it; strict charge, but no money; Abbot Hugo
would, and indeed could, give him no fraction of money.
The *Camera* in ruins, and Hugo penniless and inaccessible, Willelmus Sacrista borrowed Forty Marcs (some
Seven-and-twenty Pounds) of Benedict the Jew, and
patched up our Camera again. But the means of re-
paying him? There were no means. Hardly could
Sacrista, Cellerarius, or any public officer, get ends to
meet, on the indispensablest scale, with their shrunk
allowances: ready money had vanished.

Benedict's Twenty-seven pounds grew rapidly at
compound interest; and at length, when it had amounted
to a Hundred pounds, he, on a day of settlement,
presents the account to Hugo himself. Hugo already
owed him another Hundred of his own; and so here it
has become Two Hundred! Hugo, in a fine frenzy,
threatens to depose the Sacristan, to do this and do that;
but, in the meanwhile, How to quiet your insatiable
Jew? Hugo, for this couple of hundreds, grants the
Jew his bond for Four hundred payable at the end of
four years. At the end of four years there is, of course,
still no money; and the Jew now gets a bond for Eight
hundred and eighty pounds, to be paid by instalments,
Fourscore pounds every year. Here was a way of
doing business!

Neither yet is this insatiable Jew satisfied or settled
with: he had papers against us of 'small debts fourteen

Sacrista, Cellerarius. Low Latin, Sacristan (who looked after
the sacred vessels and vestments), and Cellarer, the official in
charge of food supplies.

years old'; his modest claim amounts finally to 'Twelve hundred pounds besides interest'—and one hopes he never got satisfied in this world; one almost hopes he was one of those beleaguered Jews who hanged themselves in York Castle shortly afterwards, and had his usances and quittances and horseleech papers summarily set fire to! For approximate justice will strive to accomplish itself; if not in one way, then in another. Jews, and also Christians and Heathens, who accumulate in this manner, though furnished with never so many parchments, do, at times, 'get their grinder-teeth successively pulled out of their head, each day a new grinder', till they consent to disgorge again. A sad fact—worth reflecting on.

Jocelin, we see, is not without secularity: Our *Dominus Abbas* was intent enough on the divine offices; but then his Account-Books—? One of the things that strike us most, throughout, in Jocelin's *Chronicle*, and indeed in Eadmer's *Anselm*, and other old monastic Books, written evidently by pious men, is this, That there is almost no mention whatever of 'personal religion' in them; that the whole gist of their thinking and speculations seems to be the 'privileges of our order', 'strict exaction of our dues', 'God's honour' (meaning the honour of our Saint), and so forth. Is not this singular? A body of men, set apart for perfecting and purifying their own souls, do not seem disturbed about that in any measure: the 'Ideal' says nothing about its idea; says much about finding bed and board for itself! How is this?

Why, for one thing, bed and board are a matter very

apt to come to speech: it is much easier to *speak* of them than of ideas; and they are sometimes much more pressing with some! Nay, for another thing, may not this religious reticence, in these devout good souls, be perhaps a merit, and sign of health in them? Jocelin, Eadmer, and such religious men, have as yet nothing of 'Methodism'; no Doubt or even root of Doubt. Religion is not a diseased self-introspection, an agonizing inquiry: their duties are clear to them, the way of supreme good plain, indisputable, and they are travelling on it. Religion lies over them like an all-embracing heavenly canopy, like an atmosphere and life-element, which is not spoken of, which in all things is pre-supposed without speech. Is not serene or complete Religion the highest aspect of human nature; as serene Cant, or complete No-religion, is the lowest and miserablest? Between which two, all manner of earnest Methodisms, introspections, agonizing inquiries, never so morbid, shall play their respective parts, not without approbation.

But let any reader fancy himself one of the Brethren in St. Edmundsbury Monastery under such circumstances! How can a Lord Abbot, all stuck-over with horseleeches of this nature, front the world? He is fast losing his life-blood, and the Convent will be as one of Pharaoh's lean kine. Old monks of experience draw their hoods deeper down; careful what they say: the monk's first duty is obedience. Our Lord the King, hearing of such work, sends down his Almoner to make investigations: but what boots it? Abbot Hugo assembles us in Chapter; asks, 'If there is any complaint?' Not a soul of us dare answer: 'Yes,

thousands!' but we all stand silent, and the Prior
even says that things are in a very comfortable condition. Whereupon old Abbot Hugo, turning to the
royal messenger, says: 'You see!'—and the business
terminates in that way. I, as a brisk-eyed noticing
youth and novice, could not help asking of the elders,
asking of Magister Samson in particular: Why he,
well-instructed and a knowing man, had not spoken out,
and brought matters to a bearing? Magister Samson
was Teacher of the Novices, appointed to breed us up to
the rules, and I loved him well. '*Fili mi*,' answered
Samson, 'the burnt child shuns the fire. Dost thou not
know, our Lord the Abbot sent me once to Acre in
Norfolk, to solitary confinement and bread-and-water,
already? The Hinghams, Hugo and Robert, have just
got home from banishment for speaking. This is the
hour of darkness: the hour when flatterers rule and are
believed. *Videat Dominus*, let the Lord see, and judge.'

In very truth, what could poor old Abbot Hugo do?
A frail old man, and the Philistines were upon him—
that is to say, the Hebrews. He had nothing for it
but to shrink away from them; get back into his warm
flannels, into his warm delusions again. Happily, before
it was quite too late, he bethought him of pilgriming to
St. Thomas of Canterbury. He set out, with a fit train,
in the autumn days of the year 1180; near Rochester
City, his mule threw him, dislocated his poor kneepan,
raised incurable inflammatory fever; and the poor old
man got his dismissal from the whole coil at once.
St. Thomas à Becket, though in a circuitous way, had

Fili mi. My son.   *Coil.* Turmoil (of life).

brought deliverance! Neither Jew usurers, nor grum-
bling monks, nor other importunate despicability of
men or mud-elements afflicted Abbot Hugo any more;
but he dropt his rosaries, closed his account-books,
closed his old eyes, and lay down into the long sleep.
Heavy-laden hoary old Dominus Hugo, fare thee well.

One thing we cannot mention without a due thrill of
horror: namely, that, in the empty exchequer of Dominus
Hugo, there was not found one penny to distribute to
the Poor that they might pray for his soul! By a kind
of godsend, Fifty shillings did, in the very nick of time,
fall due, or seem to fall due, from one of his Farmers
(the *Firmarius* de Palegrava), and he paid it, and the
Poor had it; though, alas, this too only *seemed* to fall
due, and we had it to pay again afterwards. Dominus
Hugo's apartments were plundered by his servants, to
the last portable stool, in a few minutes after the breath
was out of his body. Forlorn old Hugo, fare thee
well forever.

CHAPTER V

TWELFTH CENTURY

OUR Abbot, being dead, the *Dominus Rex*, Henry II, or
Ranulf de Glanvill *Justiciarius* of England for him, set
Inspectors or Custodiars over us—not in any breathless
haste to appoint a new Abbot, our revenues coming
into his own *Scaccarium*, or royal Exchequer, in the
mean while. They proceeded with some rigour, these
Custodiars; took written inventories, clapt-on seals,
exacted everywhere strict tale and measure: but wherefore should a living monk complain? The living monk
has to do his devotional drill-exercise; consume his
allotted *pitantia*, what we call *pittance*, or ration of
victual; and possess his soul in patience.

Dim, as through a long vista of Seven Centuries, dim
and very strange looks that monk-life to us; the ever-
surprising circumstance this, That it is a *fact* and no
dream, that we see it there, and gaze into the very eyes
of it! Smoke rises daily from those culinary chimney-
throats; there are living human beings there, who chant,
loud-braying, their matins, nones, vespers; awakening
echoes, not to the bodily ear alone. St. Edmund's
Shrine, perpetually illuminated, glows ruddy through
the Night, and through the Night of Centuries withal;
St. Edmundsbury Town paying yearly Forty pounds

for that express end. Bells clang out; on great occasions, all the bells. We have Processions, Preachings, Festivals, Christmas Plays, *Mysteries* shown in the Churchyard, at which latter the Townsfolk sometimes quarrel. Time was, Time is, as Friar Bacon's Brass Head remarked; and withal Time will be. There are three Tenses, *Tempora*, or Times; and there is one Eternity; and as for us,

We are such stuff as Dreams are made of!

Indisputable, though very dim to modern vision, rests on its hill-slope that same *Bury*, *Stow*, or Town of St. Edmund; already a considerable place, not without traffic, nay manufactures, would Jocelin only tell us what. Jocelin is totally careless of telling: but, through dim fitful apertures, we can see *Fullones*, 'Fullers', see cloth-making; looms dimly going, dye-vats, and old women spinning yarn. We have Fairs too, *Nundinæ*, in due course; and the Londoners give us much trouble, pretending that they, as a metropolitan people, are exempt from toll. Besides there is Field - husbandry, with perplexed settlement of Convent rents: corn-ricks pile themselves within burgh, in their season; and cattle depart and enter; and even the poor weaver has his cow—'dung-heaps' lying quiet at most doors (*ante foras*, says the incidental Jocelin), for the Town has yet no improved police. Watch and ward nevertheless we do keep, and have Gates—as what Town must not;

Friar Bacon's Brass Head. Roger Bacon, thirteenth-century philosopher, was said to have made a head of brass that spoke thrice; at the last words, 'Time 's past', it fell and broke.

'*We are such stuff . . .*' From *The Tempest*, Act IV sc. i.

thieves so abounding; war, *werra*, such a frequent thing!
Our thieves, at the Abbot's judgment bar, deny; claim
wager of battle; fight, are beaten, and *then* hanged.
'Ketel, the thief,' took this course; and it did nothing
for him—merely brought us, and indeed himself, new
trouble!

Everyway a most foreign Time. What difficulty, for
example, has our *Cellerarius* to collect the *repselver*,
'reaping silver', or penny, which each householder is
by law bound to pay for cutting down the Convent
grain! Richer people pretend that it is commuted, that
it is this and the other; that, in short, they will not pay
it. Our *Cellerarius* gives up calling on the rich. In the
houses of the poor, our *Cellerarius* finding, in like manner,
neither penny nor good promise, snatches, without
ceremony, what *vadium* (pledge, *wad*) he can come at:
a joint-stool, kettle, nay the very house-door, '*hostium*';
and old women, thus exposed to the unfeeling gaze of
the public, rush out after him with their distaffs and the
angriest shrieks: '*vetulæ exibant cum colis suis*,' says
Jocelin, '*minantes et exprobrantes*.'

What a historical picture, glowing visible, as St.
Edmund's Shrine by night, after Seven long Centuries
or so! *Vetulæ cum colis:* My venerable ancient spinning
grandmothers—ah, and ye too have to shriek, and rush
out with your distaffs; and become Female Chartists,
and scold all evening with void doorway; and in old
Saxon, as we in modern, would fain demand some
Five-point Charter, could it be fallen-in with, the Earth
being too tyrannous! Wise Lord Abbots, hearing of
such phenomena, did in time abolish or commute the

reap-penny, and one nuisance was abated. But the image of these justly offended old women, in their old wool costumes, with their angry features, and spindles brandished, lives forever in the historical memory. Thanks to thee, Jocelin Boswell. Jerusalem was taken by the Crusaders, and again lost by them; and Richard Cœur-de-Lion 'veiled his face' as he passed in sight of it; but how many other things went on, the while!

Thus, too, our trouble with the Lakenheath eels is very great. King Knut namely, or rather his Queen who also did herself honour by honouring St. Edmund, decreed by authentic deed yet extant on parchment, that the Holders of the Town Fields, once Beodric's, should, for one thing, go yearly and catch us four thousand eels in the marsh-pools of Lakenheath. Well, they went, they continued to go; but, in later times, got into the way of returning with a most short account of eels. Not the due six-score apiece; no, Here are two-score, Here are twenty, ten—sometimes, Here are none at all; Heaven help us, we *could* catch no more, they were not there! What is a distressed *Cellerarius* to do? We agree that each Holder of so many acres shall pay one penny yearly, and let-go the eels as too slippery. But, alas, neither is this quite effectual: the Fields, in my time, have got divided among so many hands, there is no catching of *them* either; I have known our Cellarer get seven-and-twenty pence formerly, and now it is much if he get ten pence farthing (*vix decem denarios et obolum*). And then their sheep, which they are bound to fold nightly in our pens, for the manure's sake; and, I fear, do not always fold: and their *aver-pennies*, and their *avragiums*, and their *foder-corns*, and mill-and-market dues! Thus, in its undeniable but dim manner, does old St. Edmundsbury spin and till, and laboriously keep its pot boiling, and St. Edmund's Shrine lighted, under such conditions and averages as it can.

Aver-pennies . . . avragiums. Aver-pennies were the coins payable instead of *avragium*, or day's work, which the king's tenants gave the sheriff.

Fodercorns. Fodder for the horses of a feudal lord.

CHAPTER VI

MONK SAMSON

WITHIN doors, down at the hill-foot, in our Convent here, we are a peculiar people—hardly conceivable in the Arkwright Corn-Law ages, of mere Spinning-Mills and Joe-Mantons! There is yet no Methodism among us, and we speak much of Secularities: no Methodism; our Religion is not yet a horrible restless Doubt, still less a far horribler composed Cant; but a great heaven-high Unquestionability, encompassing, interpenetrating the whole of Life. Imperfect as we may be, we are here, with our litanies, shaven crowns, vows of poverty, to testify incessantly and indisputably to every heart, That this Earthly Life and *its* riches and possessions, and good and evil hap, are not intrinsically a reality at all, but *are* a shadow of realities eternal, infinite; that this Time-world, as an air-image, fearfully *emblematic*, plays and flickers in the grand still mirror of Eternity; and man's little Life has Duties that are great, that are alone great, and go up to Heaven and down to Hell. This, with our poor litanies, we testify, and struggle to testify.

For the rest, it must be owned, we Monks of St.

Joe-Mantons. Joe Manton, 1766(?)–1835, was a famous gun-maker.

Edmundsbury are but a limited class of creatures, and
seem to have a somewhat dull life of it. Much given to
idle gossip; having indeed no other work, when our
chanting is over. Listless gossip, for most part, and a
mitigated slander; the fruit of idleness, not of spleen.
We are dull, insipid men, many of us; easy-minded;
whom prayer and digestion of food will avail for a life.
We have to receive all strangers in our Convent, and
lodge them gratis; such and such sorts go by rule to the
Lord Abbot and his special revenues; such and such to
us and our poor Cellarer, however straitened. Jews
themselves send their wives and little ones hither in
war-time, into our *Pitanceria*; where they abide safe,
with due *pittances*—for a consideration. We have the
fairest chances for collecting news. Some of us have a
turn for reading Books; for meditation, silence; at times
we even write Books. Some of us can preach, in English-
Saxon, in Norman - French, and even in Monk - Latin;
others cannot in any language or jargon, being stupid.

Failing all else, what gossip about one another! This
is a perennial resource. How one hooded head applies
itself to the ear of another, and whispers—*tacenda*.
Wilhelmus Sacrista, for instance, what does he nightly,
over in that Sacristy of his? Frequent bibations,
'*frequentes bibationes et quædam tacenda*'—eheu! We
have '*tempora minutionis*', stated seasons of blood-
letting, when we are all let blood together; and then
there is a general free-conference, a sanhedrim of clatter.
Notwithstanding our vow of poverty, we can by rule
amass to the extent of 'two shillings'; but it is to be

Tacenda. Secrets, unmentionable things.

given to our necessitous kindred, or in charity. Poor
Monks! Thus too a certain Canterbury Monk was in
the habit of 'slipping, *clanculo*, from his sleeve', five
shillings into the hand of his mother, when she came
to see him, at the divine offices, every two months.
Once, slipping the money clandestinely, just in the act
of taking leave, he slipt it not into her hand but on the
floor, and another had it; whereupon the poor Monk,
coming to know it, looked mere despair for some days;
till Lanfranc the noble Archbishop, questioning his
secret from him, nobly made the sum *seven* shillings,
and said, Never mind!

One Monk, of a taciturn nature, distinguishes himself
among these babbling ones: the name of him Samson;
he that answered Jocelin: '*Fili mi*, a burnt child shuns
the fire.' They call him 'Norfolk *Barrator*', or litigious
person; for indeed, being of grave taciturn ways, he is
not universally a favourite; he has been in trouble more
than once. The reader is desired to mark this Monk.
A personable man of seven-and-forty; stout-made,
stands erect as a pillar; with bushy eyebrows, the eyes
of him beaming into you in a really strange way;
the face massive, grave, with 'a very eminent nose';
his head almost bald, its auburn remnants of hair,
and the copious ruddy beard, getting slightly streaked
with grey. This is Brother Samson; a man worth
looking at.

He is from Norfolk, as the nickname indicates; from
Tottington in Norfolk, as we guess; the son of poor

Clanculo. Secretly.

parents there. He has told me Jocelin, for I loved him
much, That once in his ninth year he had an alarming
dream—as indeed we are all somewhat given to dreaming here. Little Samson, lying uneasily in his crib at
Tottington, dreamed that he saw the Arch Enemy in
person, just alighted in front of some grand building,
with outspread bat-wings, and stretching forth detest-
able clawed hands to grip him, little Samson, and fly off
with him: whereupon the little dreamer shrieked desperate to St. Edmund for help, shrieked and again
shrieked; and St. Edmund, a reverend heavenly figure,
did come—and indeed poor little Samson's mother,
awakened by his shrieking, did come; and the Devil
and the Dream both fled away fruitless. On the morrow,
his mother, pondering such an awful dream, thought it
were good to take him over to St. Edmund's own
Shrine, and pray with him there. See, said little
Samson at sight of the Abbey-Gate; see, mother, this
is the building I dreamed of! His poor mother dedicated
him to St. Edmund—left him there with prayers and
tears: what better could she do? The exposition of the
dream, Brother Samson used to say, was this: *Diabolus*
with outspread bat-wings shadowed forth the pleasures
of this world, *voluptates hujus sæculi*, which were about
to snatch and fly away with me, had not St. Edmund
flung his arms round me, that is to say, made me a
monk of his. A monk, accordingly, Brother Samson is;
and here to this day where his mother left him. A
learned man, of devout grave nature; has studied at
Paris, has taught in the Town Schools here, and done
much else; can preach in three languages, and, like

Dr. Caius, 'has had losses' in his time. A thoughtful,
firm-standing man; much loved by some, not loved by
all; his clear eyes flashing into you, in an almost
inconvenient way!

Abbot Hugo, as we said, had his own difficulties with
him; Abbot Hugo had him in prison once, to teach him
what authority was, and how to dread the fire in future.
For Brother Samson, in the time of the Antipopes, had
been sent to Rome on business; and, returning successful,
was too late—the business had all misgone in the interim!
As tours to Rome are still frequent with us English,
perhaps the reader will not grudge to look at the method
of travelling thither in those remote ages. We happily
have, in small compass, a personal narrative of it.
Through the clear eyes and memory of Brother Samson
one peeps direct into the very bosom of that Twelfth
Century, and finds it rather curious. The actual *Papa*,
Father, or universal President of Christendom, as yet not
grown chimerical, sat there; think of that only! Brother
Samson went to Rome as to the real Light-fountain of
this lower world; we now—! But let us hear Brother
Samson, as to his mode of travelling:

'You know what trouble I had for that Church of
Woolpit; how I was dispatched to Rome in the time of
the Schism between Pope Alexander and Octavian;
and passed through Italy at that season, when all clergy
carrying letters for our Lord Pope Alexander were laid
hold of, and some were clapt in prison, some hanged;

Dr. Caius. Physician in *The Merry Wives of Windsor*; but
the words quoted refer to Dogberry in *Much Ado About Nothing*.
Octavian. Antipope during the papacy of Alexander III.

and some, with nose and lips cut off, were sent forward
to our Lord the Pope, for the disgrace and confusion
of him (*in dedecus et confusionem ejus*). I, however,
pretended to be Scotch, and putting on the garb of a
Scotchman, and taking the gesture of one, walked along;
and when anybody mocked at me, I would brandish my
staff in the manner of that weapon they call *gaveloc*,
uttering comminatory words after the way of the
Scotch. To those that met and questioned me who
I was, I made no answer but: *Ride, ride Rome; turne
Cantwereberei.* Thus did I, to conceal myself and my
errand, and get safer to Rome under the guise of a
Scotchman.

'Having at last obtained a Letter from our Lord the
Pope according to my wishes, I turned homewards
again. I had to pass through a certain strong town on
my road; and lo, the soldiers thereof surrounded me,
seizing me, and saying: "This vagabond (*iste solivagus*),
who pretends to be Scotch, is either a spy, or has Letters
from the false Pope Alexander.' And whilst they
examined every stitch and rag of me, my leggings
(*caligas*), breeches, and even the old shoes that I carried
over my shoulder in the way of the Scotch—I put my
hand into the leather scrip I wore, wherein our Lord
the Pope's Letter lay, close by a little jug (*ciffus*) I had
for drinking out of; and the Lord God so pleasing, and
St. Edmund, I got out both the Letter and the jug

Gaveloc. Javelin or dart.
Ride, ride Rome, etc. 'Rome forever; Canterbury *not*'
(Carlyle's conjecture); but it may mean: 'I ride towards Rome,
turning from Canterbury' (i.e. 'I give no allegiance to Alexander').

together; in such a way that, extending my arm aloft,
I held the Letter hidden between jug and hand: they
saw the jug, but the Letter they saw not. And thus
I escaped out of their hands in the name of the Lord.
Whatever money I had, they took from me; wherefore I
had to beg from door to door, without any payment (*sine
omni expensa*) till I came to England again. But hearing
that the Woolpit Church was already given to Geoffry
Ridell, my soul was struck with sorrow because I had
laboured in vain. Coming home, therefore, I sat me
down secretly under the Shrine of St. Edmund, fearing
lest our Lord Abbot should seize and imprison me, though
I had done no mischief; nor was there a monk who durst
speak to me, nor a laic who durst bring me food except
by stealth.'

Such resting and welcoming found Brother Samson,
with his worn soles, and strong heart! He sits silent,
revolving many thoughts, at the foot of St. Edmund's
Shrine. In the wide Earth, if it be not Saint Edmund,
what friend or refuge has he? Our Lord Abbot, hearing
of him, sent the proper officer to lead him down to
prison, and clap 'foot-gyves on him' there. Another
poor official furtively brought him a cup of wine; bade
him 'be comforted in the Lord'. Samson utters no
complaint; obeys in silence. 'Our Lord Abbot, taking
counsel of it, banished me to Acre, and there I had to
stay long.'

Our Lord Abbot next tried Samson with promotions;
made him Subsacristan; made him Librarian, which he
liked best of all, being passionately fond of Books:
Samson, with many thoughts in him, again obeyed in

silence; discharged his offices to perfection, but never
thanked our Lord Abbot—seemed rather as if looking
into him, with those clear eyes of his. Whereupon
Abbot Hugo said, *Se nunquam vidisse*, He had never
seen such a man; whom no severity would break to
complain, and no kindness soften into smiles or thanks
—a questionable kind of man!

In this way, not without troubles, but still in an erect
clear-standing manner, has Brother Samson reached his
forty-seventh year; and his ruddy beard is getting
slightly grizzled. He is endeavouring, in these days, to
have various broken things thatched in; nay perhaps to
have the Choir itself completed, for he can bear nothing
ruinous. He has gathered 'heaps of lime and sand';
has masons, slaters working, he and *Warinus monachus
noster*, who are joint keepers of the Shrine; paying out
the money duly—furnished by charitable burghers of
St. Edmundsbury, they say. Charitable burghers of
St. Edmundsbury? To me Jocelin it seems rather,
Samson, and Warinus whom he leads, have privily
hoarded the oblations at the Shrine itself, in these late
years of indolent dilapidation, while Abbot Hugo sat
wrapt inaccessible; and are struggling, in this prudent
way, to have the rain kept out! Under what conditions,
sometimes, has Wisdom to struggle with Folly; get
Folly persuaded to so much as thatch out the rain from
itself! For, indeed, if the Infant govern the Nurse,
what dextrous practice on the Nurse's part will not be
necessary!

It is a new regret to us that, in these circumstances,
our Lord the King's Custodiars, interfering, prohibited

all building or thatching from whatever source; and no Choir shall be completed, and Rain and Time, for the present, shall have their way. Willelmus Sacrista, he of 'the frequent bibations and some things not to be spoken of'; he, with his red nose, I am of opinion, had made complaint to the Custodiars; wishing to do Samson an ill turn—Samson his *Sub*-sacristan, with those clear eyes, could not be a prime favourite of his! Samson again obeys in silence.

CHAPTER VII

THE CANVASSING

Now, however, come great news to St. Edmundsbury:
That there is to be an Abbot elected; that our interlunar
obscuration is to cease; St. Edmund's Convent no more
to be a doleful widow, but joyous and once again a bride!
Often in our widowed state had we prayed to the Lord
and St. Edmund, singing weekly a matter of 'one-and-
twenty penitential Psalms, on our knees in the Choir',
that a fit Pastor might be vouchsafed us.   And, says
Jocelin, had some known what Abbot we were to get,
they had not been so devout, I believe!   Bozzy Jocelin
opens to mankind the floodgates of authentic Convent
gossip; we listen, as in a Dionysius' Ear, to the inanest
hubbub, like the voices at Virgil's Horn-Gate of Dreams.
Even gossip, seven centuries off, has significance.   List,
list, how like men are to one another in all centuries.

'*Dixit quidam de quodam*, A certain person said of a
certain person: "He, that *Frater*, is a good monk, *pro-*

Dionysius' Ear. A vast cavern, shaped like an ear, and
having curious acoustic properties, near Syracuse in Sicily.
Tradition says that Dionysius the Tyrant (died 367 B.C.) built it
as a prison, so that he could hear the smallest whispers of his
victims.

Horn-Gate of Dreams. Virgil tells of two gates, one of horn,
through which came true dreams, the other of ivory, whence
came false ones (*Æneid* vi).

babilis persona; knows much of the order and customs of the church; and, though not so perfect a philosopher as some others, would make a very good Abbot. Old Abbot Ording, still famed among us, knew little of letters. Besides, as we read in Fables, it is better to choose a log for king, than a serpent never so wise, that will venomously hiss and bite his subjects." "Impossible!" answered the other: "How can such a man make a sermon in the Chapter, or to the people on festival-days, when he is without letters? How can he have the skill to bind and to loose, he who does not understand the Scriptures? How—?" '

And then 'another said of another, *alius de alio*: "That *Frater* is a *homo literatus*, eloquent, sagacious; vigorous in discipline; loves the Convent much, has suffered much for its sake.' To which a third party answers: "From all your great clerks, good Lord deliver us! From Norfolk barrators and surly persons, That it would please thee to preserve us, We beseech thee to hear us, good Lord!" Then another *quidam* said of another *quodam*: "That *Frater* is a good manager (*husebondus*)"; but was swiftly answered: "God forbid that a man who can neither read nor chant, nor celebrate the divine offices, an unjust person withal, and grinder of the faces of the poor, should ever be Abbot!" ' One man, it appears, is nice in his victuals. Another is indeed wise, but apt to slight inferiors; hardly at the pains to answer, if they argue with him too foolishly. And so each *aliquis* concerning his *aliquo*—through whole pages of electioneering babble. 'For,' says Jocelin, 'So many men, as many minds.' Our Monks

'at time of blood-letting, *tempore minutionis*', holding
their sanhedrim of babble, would talk in this manner:
Brother Samson, I remarked, never said anything; sat
silent, sometimes smiling; but he took good note of what
others said, and would bring it up, on occasion, twenty
years after. As for me Jocelin, I was of opinion that
'some skill in Dialectics, to distinguish true from false',
would be good in an Abbot. I spake, as a rash Novice
in those days, some conscientious words of a certain
benefactor of mine; 'and behold, one of those sons of
Belial' ran and reported them to him, so that he never
after looked at me with the same face again! Poor
Bozzy!

Such is the buzz and frothy simmering ferment of
the general mind and no-mind; struggling to 'make
itself up', as the phrase is, or ascertain what *it* does
really want: no easy matter, in most cases. St.
Edmundsbury, in that Candlemas season of the year
1182, is a busily fermenting place. The very cloth-
makers sit meditative at their looms; asking, Who shall
be Abbot? The *sochemanni* speak of it, driving their
ox-teams afield; the old women with their spindles: and
none yet knows what the days will bring forth.

The Prior, however, as our interim chief, must proceed
to work; get ready 'Twelve Monks', and set off with
them to his Majesty at Waltham, there shall the election
be made. An election, whether managed directly by
ballot-box on public hustings, or indirectly by force of

Sochemanni. Socmen, tenants who hold land by socage, a
special form of service.

public opinion, or were it even by open alehouses, land-lords' coercion, popular club-law, or whatever electoral methods, is always an interesting phenomenon. A mountain tumbling in great travail, throwing up dust-clouds and absurd noises, is visibly there; uncertain yet what mouse or monster it will give birth to.

Besides, it is a most important social act; nay, at bottom, the one important social act. Given the men a People choose, the People itself, in its exact worth and worthlessness, is given. A heroic people chooses heroes, and is happy; a valet or flunkey people chooses sham-heroes, what are called quacks, thinking them heroes, and is not happy. The grand summary of a man's spiritual condition, what brings out all his herohood and insight, or all his flunkeyhood and horn-eyed dimness, is this question put to him, What man dost thou honour? Which is thy ideal of a man; or nearest that? So too of a People: for a People too, every People, *speaks* its choice—were it only by silently obeying, and not revolt-ing—in the course of a century or so. Nor are electoral methods, Reform Bills and such-like, unimportant. A People's electoral methods are, in the long run, the express image of its electoral *talent*; tending and gravi-tating perpetually, irresistibly, to a conformity with that: and are, at all stages, very significant of the People. Judicious readers, of these times, are not dis-inclined to see how Monks elect their Abbot in the Twelfth Century: how the St. Edmundsbury mountain manages its midwifery; and what mouse or man the outcome is.

CHAPTER VIII

THE ELECTION

ACCORDINGLY our Prior assembles us in Chapter; and we adjuring him before God to do justly, nominates, not by our selection, yet with our assent, Twelve Monks, moderately satisfactory. Of whom are Hugo Third-Prior, Brother Dennis a venerable man, Walter the *Medicus*, Samson *Subsacrista*, and other esteemed characters—though Willelmus *Sacrista*, of the red nose, too is one. These shall proceed straightway to Waltham; and there elect the Abbot as they may and can. Monks are sworn to obedience; must not speak too loud, under penalty of foot-gyves, limbo, and bread-and-water: yet monks too would know what it is they are obeying. The St. Edmundsbury Community has no hustings, ballot-box, indeed no open voting: yet by various vague manipulations, pulse-feelings, we struggle to ascertain what its virtual aim is, and succeed better or worse.

This question, however, rises; alas, a quite preliminary question: Will the *Dominus Rex* allow us to choose freely? It is to be hoped! Well, if so, we agree to choose one of our own Convent. If not, if the *Dominus Rex* will force a stranger on us, we decide on demurring, the Prior and his Twelve shall demur: we can appeal, plead, remonstrate; appeal even to the Pope, but trust it will not be necessary. Then there is this other question, raised by Brother Samson: What if the Thirteen should not themselves be able to agree? Brother Samson *Subsacrista*, one remarks, is ready oftenest with some question, some suggestion, that has wisdom in it. Though a servant of servants, and saying little, his words all tell, having sense in them; it seems by his light mainly that we steer ourselves in this great dimness.

What if the Thirteen should not themselves be able to agree? Speak, Samson, and advise. Could not, hints Samson, Six of our venerablest elders be chosen by us, a kind of electoral committee, here and now: of these, 'with their hand on the Gospels, with their eye on the *Sacrosancta*', we take oath that they will do faithfully; let these, in secret and as before God, agree on Three whom they reckon fittest; write their names in a Paper, and deliver the same sealed, forthwith, to the Thirteen: one of those Three the Thirteen shall fix on, if permitted. If not permitted, that is to say, if the *Dominus Rex* force us to demur—the paper shall be brought back unopened, and publicly burned, that no man's secret bring him into trouble.

So Samson advises, so we act; wisely, in this and in other crises of the business. Our electoral committee, its eye on the Sacrosancta, is soon named, soon sworn; and we, striking up the Fifth Psalm, '*Verba mea*',

> 'Give ear unto my words, O Lord,
> My meditation weigh,'

march out chanting, and leave the Six to their work

Sacrosancta. Consecrated elements used in the Mass.

in the Chapter here. Their work, before long, they
announce as finished: they, with their eye on the Sacrosancta, imprecating the Lord to weigh and witness
their meditation, have fixed on Three Names, and
written them in this Sealed Paper. Let Samson Subsacrista, general servant of the party, take charge of
it. On the morrow morning, our Prior and his Twelve
will be ready to get under way.

This, then, is the ballot-box and electoral winnowing-
machine they have at St. Edmundsbury: a mind fixed
on the Thrice Holy, an appeal to God on high to witness
their meditation: by far the best, and indeed the only
good electoral winnowing-machine—if men have souls
in them. Totally worthless, it is true, and even hideous
and poisonous, if men have no souls. But without soul,
alas, what winnowing-machine in human elections can
be of avail? We cannot get along without soul; we
stick fast, the mournfulest spectacle; and salt itself
will not save us!

On the morrow morning, accordingly, our Thirteen
set forth; or rather our Prior and Eleven; for Samson,
as general servant of the party, has to linger, settling
many things. At length he too gets upon the road;
and, 'carrying the sealed Paper in a leather pouch hung
round his neck; and *froccum bajulans in ulnis*' (thanks
to thee, Bozzy Jocelin), 'his frock-skirts looped over
his elbow', showing substantial stern-works, tramps
stoutly along. Away across the Heath, not yet of
Newmarket and horse-jockeying; across your Fleam-

Imprecating. Used here for *invoking*.

dike and Devil's-dike, no longer useful as a Mercian
East-Anglian boundary or bulwark: continually towards
Waltham, and the Bishop of Winchester's House there,
for his Majesty is in that. Brother Samson, as purse-
bearer, has the reckoning always, when there is one, to
pay; 'delays are numerous', progress none of the swiftest.

But, in the solitude of the Convent, Destiny thus big
and in her birthtime, what gossiping, what babbling,
what dreaming of dreams! The secret of the Three
our electoral elders alone know: some Abbot we shall
have to govern us; but which Abbot, oh, which! One
Monk discerns in a vision of the night-watches, that we
shall get an Abbot of our own body, without needing to
demur: a prophet appeared to him clad all in white,
and said: 'Ye shall have one of yours, and he will rage
among you like a wolf, *sæviet ut lupus.*' Verily!—then
which of ours? Another Monk now dreams: he has
seen clearly which; a certain Figure taller by head and
shoulders than the other two, dressed in alb and *pallium*,
and with the attitude of one about to fight—which tall .
Figure a wise Editor would rather not name at this
stage of the business! Enough that the vision is true:
that Saint Edmund himself, pale and awful, seemed to
rise from his Shrine, with naked feet, and say audibly:
'He, *ille*, shall veil my feet'; which part of the vision
also proves true. Such guessing, visioning, dim perscrutation of the momentous future: the very cloth-
makers, old women, all townsfolk speak of it, 'and more
than once it is reported in St. Edmundsbury, This one

Perscrutation. Literally, thorough investigation; here seems to
mean penetration.

is elected; and then, This one, and That other'.   Who
knows?

But now, sure enough, at Waltham 'on the second
Sunday of Quadragesima', which Dryasdust declares
to mean the 22d day of February, year 1182, Thirteen
St. Edmundsbury Monks are, at last, seen processioning
towards the Winchester Manorhouse; and, in some high
Presence-chamber and Hall of State, get access to
Henry II in all his glory.   What a Hall—not imaginary
in the least, but entirely real and indisputable, though
so extremely dim to us; sunk in the deep distances of
Night!   The Winchester Manorhouse has fled bodily,
like a Dream of the old Night; not Dryasdust himself
can show a wreck of it.   House and people, royal and
episcopal, lords and varlets, where are they?   Why
there, I say, Seven Centuries off; sunk *so* far in the
Night, there they *are*; peep through the blankets of the
old Night, and thou wilt see!   King Henry himself is
visibly there; a vivid, noble-looking man, with grizzled
beard, in glittering uncertain costume; with earls round
him, and bishops, and dignitaries, in the like.   The
Hall is large, and has for one thing an altar near it—
chapel and altar adjoining it; but what gilt seats, carved
tables, carpeting of rush-cloth, what arras-hangings,
and huge fire of logs—alas, it has Human Life in it;
and is not that the grand miracle, in what hangings
or costume soever?

Wreck. Carlyle seems to have in mind the *Tempest* passage
quoted before (p. 43) and to confuse 'wreck' (or 'wrack') with
'rack', used of the filmy upper clouds.   Editors of Shakespeare
in Carlyle's time are probably responsible for the error.

The *Dominus Rex*, benignantly receiving our Thirteen with their obeisance, and graciously declaring that he will strive to act for God's honour and the Church's good, commands, 'by the Bishop of Winchester and Geoffrey the Chancellor'—*Galfridus Cancellarius*, Henry's and the Fair Rosamond's authentic Son present here!—commands: 'That they, the said Thirteen, do now withdraw, and fix upon Three from their own Monastery.' A work soon done; the Three hanging ready round Samson's neck, in that leather pouch of his. Breaking the seal, we find the names—what think *ye* of it, ye higher dignitaries, thou indolent Prior, thou Willelmus *Sacrista* with the red bottle-nose?—the names, in this order: of Samson *Subsacrista*, of Roger the distressed Cellarer, of Hugo *Tertius-Prior*.

The higher dignitaries, all omitted here, 'flush suddenly red in the face', but have nothing to say. One curious fact and question certainly is, How Hugo Third-Prior, who was of the electoral committee, came to nominate *himself* as one of the Three? A curious fact, which Hugo Third-Prior has never yet entirely explained, that I know of! However, we return, and report to the King our Three names; merely altering the order; putting Samson last, as lowest of all. The King, at recitation of our Three, asks us: 'Who are they? Were they born in my domain? Totally unknown to me! You must nominate three others.' Whereupon Willelmus Sacrista says: 'Our Prior must be named, *quia caput nostrum est*, being already our head.' And the

---

Fair Rosamond. Rosamund Clifford, said to have been the mother of Geoffrey the Chancellor.

Prior responds: 'Willelmus Sacrista is a fit man, *bonus vir est*'—for all his red nose. Tickle me, Toby, and I 'll tickle thee! Venerable Dennis too is named; none in his conscience can say nay. There are now Six on our List. 'Well,' said the King, 'they have done it swiftly, they! *Deus est cum eis.*' The Monks withdraw again; and Majesty revolves, for a little, with his *Pares* and *Episcopi*, Lords or '*Law-wards*' and Soul-Overseers, the thoughts of the royal breast. The Monks wait silent in an outer room.

In short while, they are next ordered, To add yet another three; but not from their own Convent; from other Convents, 'for the honour of my kingdom'. Here —what is to be done here? We will demur, if need be! We do name three, however, for the nonce: the Prior of St. Faith's, a good Monk of St. Neot's, a good Monk of St. Alban's; good men all; all made abbots and dignitaries since, at this hour. There are now Nine upon our List. What the thoughts of the Dominus Rex may be farther? The Dominus Rex, thanking graciously, sends out word that we shall now strike off three. The three strangers are instantly struck off. Willelmus Sacrista adds, that he will of his own accord decline—a touch of grace and respect for the *Sacrosancta*, even in Willelmus! The King then orders us to strike off a couple more; then yet one more: Hugo Third Prior goes, and Roger *Cellerarius*, and venerable Monk Dennis—and now there

---

Pares and Episcopi. Peers and Bishops.
Law-wards. Not the true origin of 'lord', which is derived from Anglo-Saxon 'hlaford', from probably 'hlaf weard', i.e. 'loaf (bread) ward'.

remain on our List two only, Samson Subsacrista and the Prior.

Which of these two? It were hard to say—by Monks who may get themselves foot-gyved and thrown into limbo for speaking! We humbly request that the Bishop of Winchester and Geoffrey the Chancellor may again enter, and help us to decide. 'Which do you want?' asks the Bishop. Venerable Dennis made a speech, 'commending the persons of the Prior and Samson; but always in the corner of his discourse, *in angulo sui sermonis*, brought Samson in'. 'I see!' said the Bishop: 'We are to understand that your Prior is somewhat remiss; that you want to have him you call Samson for Abbot.' 'Either of them is good,' said venerable Dennis, almost trembling; 'but we would have the better, if it pleased God.' 'Which of the two *do* you want?' inquires the Bishop pointedly. 'Samson!' answered Dennis; 'Samson!' echoed all of the rest that durst speak or echo anything: and Samson is reported to the King accordingly. His Majesty, advising of it for a moment, orders that Samson be brought in with the other Twelve.

The King's Majesty, looking at us somewhat sternly, then says: 'You present to me Samson; I do not know him: had it been your Prior, whom I do know, I should have accepted him: however, I will now do as you wish. But have a care of yourselves. By the true eyes of God, *per veros oculos Dei*, if you manage badly, I will be upon you!' Samson, therefore, steps forward, kisses the King's feet; but swiftly rises erect again, swiftly turns towards the altar, uplifting with the other Twelve, in clear tenor-note, the Fifty-first Psalm, '*Miserere mei Deus*',

> 'After thy loving-kindness, Lord,
> Have mercy upon *me*;'

with firm voice, firm step and head, no change in his countenance whatever. 'By God's eyes,' said the King, 'that one, I think, will govern the Abbey well.' By the same oath (charged to your Majesty's account), I too am precisely of that opinion! It is some while since I fell in with a likelier man anywhere than this new Abbot Samson. Long life to him, and may the Lord *have* mercy on him as Abbot!

Thus, then, have the St. Edmundsbury Monks, without express ballot-box or other good winnowing-machine, contrived to accomplish the most important social feat a body of men can do, to winnow out the man that is to govern them: and truly one sees not that, by any winnowing-machine whatever, they could have done it better.

CHAPTER IX

ABBOT SAMSON

So, then, the bells of St. Edmundsbury clang out one and all, and in church and chapel the organs go: Convent and Town, and all the west side of Suffolk, are in gala; knights, viscounts, weavers, spinners, the entire population, male and female, young and old, the very sockmen with their chubby infants—out to have a holiday, and see the Lord Abbot arrive! And there is 'stripping barefoot' of the Lord Abbot at the Gate, and solemn leading of him in to the High Altar and Shrine; with sudden 'silence of all the bells and organs', as we kneel in deep prayer there; and again with outburst of all the bells and organs, and loud *Te Deum* from the general human windpipe; and speeches by the leading viscount, and giving of the kiss of brotherhood; the whole wound up with popular games, and dinner within doors of more than a thousand strong, *plus quam mille comedentibus in gaudio magno*.

In such manner is the selfsame Samson once again returning to us, welcomed on *this* occasion. He that went away with his frock-skirts looped over his arm, comes back riding high; suddenly made one of the dignitaries of this world. Reflective readers will admit that here was a trial for a man. Yesterday a poor mendicant, allowed to possess not above two shillings of

Plus quam mille. . . . More than a thousand feasting together in great joy.

money, and without authority to bid a dog run for him
—this man to-day finds himself a *Dominus Abbas*,
mitred Peer of Parliament, Lord of manorhouses, farms,
manors, and wide lands; a man with 'Fifty Knights
under him', and dependent, swiftly obedient multitudes
of men. It is a change greater than Napoleon's; so
sudden withal. As if one of the Chandos day-drudges
had, on awakening some morning, found that *he* over-
night was become Duke! Let Samson with his clear-
beaming eyes see into that, and discern it if he can.
We shall now get the measure of him by a new scale of
inches, considerably more rigorous than the former was.
For if a noble soul is rendered tenfold beautifuler by
victory and prosperity, springing now radiant as into
his own due element and sun-throne; an ignoble one
is rendered tenfold and hundredfold uglier, pitifuler.
Whatsoever vices, whatsoever weaknesses were in the
man, the parvenu will show us them enlarged, as in
the solar microscope, into frightful distortion. Nay,
how many mere seminal principles of vice, hitherto all
wholesomely kept latent, may we now see unfolded, as
in the solar hothouse, into growth, into huge universally-
conspicuous luxuriance and development!

Abbot Samson had found a Convent all in dilapidation;
rain beating through it, material rain and metaphorical,
from all quarters of the compass. Willelmus Sacrista sits
drinking nightly, and doing mere *tacenda*. Our larders

Chandos. The Duke of Chandos, taken as a typical nobleman.
Solar microscope. A magic lantern in which the light of the
sun was used instead of a lamp.

are reduced to leanness, Jew harpies and unclean
creatures our purveyors; in our basket is no bread.
Old women with their distaffs rush out on a distressed
Cellarer in shrill Chartism. 'You cannot stir abroad
but Jews and Christians pounce upon you with un-
settled bonds'; debts boundless seemingly as the
National Debt of England. For four years our new
Lord Abbot never went abroad but Jew creditors and
Christian, and all manner of creditors, were about him;
driving him to very despair. Our Prior is remiss; our
Cellarers, officials are remiss; our monks are remiss;
what man is not remiss? Front this, Samson, thou
alone art there to front it; it is thy task to front and
fight this, and to die or kill it. May the Lord have
mercy on thee!

To our antiquarian interest in poor Jocelin and his
Convent, where the whole aspect of existence, the whole
dialect, of thought, of speech, of activity, is so obsolete,
strange, long-vanished, there now superadds itself a
mild glow of human interest for Abbot Samson; a real
pleasure, as at sight of man's work, especially of governing, which is man's highest work, done *well*. Abbot
Samson had no experience in governing; had served no
apprenticeship to the trade of governing—alas, only the
hardest apprenticeship to that of obeying. He had
never in any court given *vadium* or *plegium*, says Jocelin;
hardly ever seen a court, when he was set to preside in
one. But it is astonishing, continues Jocelin, how soon
he learned the ways of business; and, in all sorts of
affairs, became expert beyond others. Of the many

Vadium or plegium. A pledge or bail to reappear in court.

persons offering him their service, 'he retained one
Knight skilled in taking *vadia* and *plegia*'; and within
the year was himself well skilled. Nay, by and by, the
Pope appoints him Justiciary in certain causes; the
King one of his new Circuit Judges: official Osbert is
heard saying: 'That Abbot is one of your shrewd ones,
disputator est; if he go on as he·begins, he will cut out
every lawyer of us!'

Why not? What is to hinder this Samson from
governing? There is in him what far transcends all
apprenticeships; in the man himself there exists a model
of governing, something to govern by! There exists in
him a heart-abhorrence of whatever is incoherent, pusil-
lanimous, unveracious—that is to say, chaotic, *un*-
governed; of the Devil, not of God. A man of this
kind cannot help governing! He has the living ideal
of a governor in him; and the incessant necessity of
struggling to unfold the same out of him. Not the
Devil or Chaos, for any wages, will he serve; no, this
man is the born servant of Another than them. Alas,
how little avail all apprenticeships, when there is in
your governor himself what we may well call *nothing* to
govern by: nothing—a general grey twilight, looming
with shapes of expediencies, parliamentary traditions,
division-lists, election-funds, leading-articles; this, with
what of vulpine alertness and adroitness soever, is
not much!

But indeed what say we, apprenticeship? Had not
this Samson served, in his way, a right good apprenticeship to governing; namely, the harshest slave-appren-
ticeship to obeying! Walk this world with no friend

in it but God and St. Edmund, you will either fall into the ditch, or learn a good many things. To learn obeying is the fundamental art of governing. How much would many a Serene Highness have learned, had he travelled through the world with water-jug and empty wallet, *sine omni expensa*; and, at his victorious return, sat down not to newspaper-paragraphs and city-illuminations, but at the foot of St. Edmund's Shrine to shackles and bread-and-water! He that cannot be servant of many, will never be master, true guide and deliverer of many—that is the meaning of true mastership. Had not the Monk-life extraordinary 'political capabilities' in it; if not imitable by us, yet enviable? Heavens, had a Duke of Logwood, now rolling sumptuously to his place in the Collective Wisdom, but himself happened to plough daily, at one time, on seven-and-sixpence a week, with no outdoor relief—what a light, unquenchable by logic and statistic and arithmetic, would it have thrown on several things for him!

Sine omni expensa. Without any expense; living on charity.

CHAPTER X

GOVERNMENT

How Abbot Samson, giving his new subjects seriatim
the kiss of fatherhood in the St. Edmundsbury chapter-
house, proceeded with cautious energy to set about
reforming their disjointed distracted way of life; how
he managed with his Fifty rough *Milites* (Feudal
Knights), with his lazy Farmers, remiss refractory
Monks, with Pope's Legates, Viscounts, Bishops, Kings;
how on all sides he laid about him like a man, and putting
consequence on premiss, and everywhere the saddle on
the right horse, struggled incessantly to educe organic
method out of lazily fermenting wreck—the careful
reader will discern, not without true interest, in these
pages of Jocelin Boswell. In most antiquarian quaint
costume, not of garments alone, but of thought, word,
action, outlook, and position, the substantial figure of
a man with eminent nose, bushy brows, and clear-
flashing eyes, his russet beard growing daily greyer, is
visible, engaged in true governing of men.   It is beautiful
how the chrysalis governing-soul, shaking off its dusty
slough and prison, starts forth winged, a true royal
soul! Our new Abbot has a right honest unconscious

Putting consequence on premiss. Drawing the right conclusion
from *premises* or data.

feeling, without insolence as without fear or flutter, of what he is and what others are. A courage to quell the proudest, an honest pity to encourage the humblest. Withal there is a noble reticence in this Lord Abbot: much vain unreason he hears; lays up without response. He is not there to expect reason and nobleness of others; he is there to give them of his own reason and nobleness. Is he not their servant, as we said, who can suffer from them, and for them; bear the burden their poor spindle-limbs totter and stagger under; and, in virtue of *being* their servant, govern them, lead them out of weakness into strength, out of defeat into victory!

One of the first Herculean Labours Abbot Samson undertook, or the very first, was to institute a strenuous review and radical reform of his economics. It is the first labour of every governing man, from *Paterfamilias* to *Dominus Rex*. To get the rain thatched out from you is the preliminary of whatever farther, in the way of speculation or of action, you may mean to do. Old Abbot Hugo's budget, as we saw, had become empty, filled with deficit and wind. To see his account-books clear, be delivered from those ravening flights of Jew and Christian creditors, pouncing on him like obscene harpies wherever he showed face, was a necessity for Abbot Samson.

On the morrow after his instalment he brings in a load of money-bonds, all duly stamped, sealed with this or the other Convent Seal: frightful, unmanageable, a bottomless confusion of Convent finance. There they are—but there at least they all are; all that shall be

of them.   Our Lord Abbot demands that all the official
seals in use among us be now produced and delivered
to him.   Three-and-thirty seals turn up; are straightway broken, and shall seal no more: the Abbot only,
and those duly authorized by him shall seal any bond.
There are but two ways of paying debt: increase of
industry in raising income, increase of thrift in laying
it out.   With iron energy, in slow but steady unde-
viating perseverance, Abbot Samson sets to work in
both directions.   His troubles are manifold: cunning
milites, unjust bailiffs, lazy sockmen, he an inexperienced
Abbot; relaxed lazy monks, not disinclined to mutiny
in mass: but continued vigilance, rigorous method,
what we call 'the eye of the master', work wonders.
The clear-beaming eyesight of Abbot Samson, steadfast,
severe, all-penetrating—it is like *Fiat lux* in that inorganic waste whirlpool; penetrates gradually to all
nooks, and of the chaos makes a *kosmos* or ordered world!

He arranges everywhere, struggles unweariedly to
arrange, and place on some intelligible footing, the
'affairs and dues, *res ac redditus*', of his dominion.   The
Lakenheath eels cease to breed squabbles between
human beings; the penny of *reap-silver* to explode
into the streets the Female Chartism of St. Edmundsbury.   These and innumerable greater things.   Wheresoever Disorder may stand or lie, let it have a care;
here is the man that has declared war with it, that
never will make peace with it.   Man is the Missionary
of Order; he is the servant not of the Devil and Chaos,

Reap-silver. Money payment in lieu of harvest work due
from a feudal tenant.   See p. 44.

but of God and the Universe! Let all sluggards and cowards, remiss, false-spoken, unjust, and otherwise diabolic persons have a care: this is a dangerous man for them. He has a mild grave face; a thoughtful sternness, a sorrowful pity: but there is a terrible flash of anger in him too; lazy monks often have to murmur: '*Sævit ut lupus*, He rages like a wolf; was not our Dream true!' 'To repress and hold-in such sudden anger he was continually careful,' and succeeded well: right, Samson; that it may become in thee as noble central heat, fruitful, strong, beneficent; not blaze out, or the seldomest possible blaze out, as wasteful volcanoism to scorch and consume!

'We must first creep, and gradually learn to walk,' had Abbot Samson said of himself, at starting. In four years he had become a great walker; striding prosperously along; driving much before him. In less than four years, says Jocelin, the Convent Debts were all liquidated: the harpy Jews not only settled with, but banished, bag and baggage, out of the *Bannaleuca* (Liberties, *Banlieue*) of St. Edmundsbury—so has the King's Majesty been persuaded to permit. Farewell to *you*, at any rate; let us, in no extremity, apply again to you! Armed men march them over the borders, dismiss them under stern penalties—sentence of excommunication on all that shall again harbour them here: there were many dry eyes at their departure.

New life enters everywhere, springs up beneficent, the Incubus of Debt once rolled away. Samson hastes not; but neither does he pause to rest. This of the Finance

is a lifelong business with him—Jocelin's anecdotes are
filled to weariness with it. As indeed to Jocelin it was
of very primary interest.

But we have to record also, with a lively satisfaction,
that spiritual rubbish is as little tolerated in Samson's
Monastery as material. With due rigour, Willelmus
Sacrista, and his bibations and *tacenda* are, at the earliest
opportunity, softly yet irrevocably put an end to. The
bibations, namely, had to end; even the building where
they used to be carried on was razed from the soil of
St. Edmundsbury, and 'on its place grow rows of
beans': Willelmus himself, deposed from the Sacristy
and all offices, retires into obscurity, into absolute
taciturnity unbroken thenceforth to this hour. Whether
the poor Willelmus did not still, by secret channels,
occasionally get some slight wetting of vinous or alco-
holic liquor—now grown, in a manner, indispensable to the poor man? Jocelin hints not; one knows not how
to hope, what to hope! But if he did, it was in silence
and darkness; with an ever-present feeling that tee-
totalism was his only true course. Drunken dissolute
Monks are a class of persons who had better keep out
of Abbot Samson's way. *Sævit ut lupus*; was not the
Dream true! murmured many a Monk. Nay Ranulf de
Glanvill, Justiciary in Chief, took umbrage at him,
seeing these strict ways; and watched farther with
suspicion: but discerned gradually that there was
nothing wrong, that there was much the opposite of
wrong.

CHAPTER XI

THE ABBOT'S WAYS

ABBOT SAMSON showed no extraordinary favour to the Monks who had been his familiars of old; did not promote them to offices—*nisi essent idonei*, unless they chanced to be fit men! Whence great discontent among certain of these, who had contributed to make him Abbot: reproaches, open and secret, of his being 'ungrateful, hard-tempered, unsocial, a Norfolk *barrator* and *paltenerius*'.

Indeed, except it were for *idonei*, 'fit men', in all kinds, it was hard to say for whom Abbot Samson had much favour. He loved his kindred well, and tenderly enough acknowledged the poor part of them; with the rich part, who in old days had never acknowledged him, he totally refused to have any business. But even the former he did not promote into offices; finding none of them *idonei*. 'Some whom he thought suitable he put into situations in his own household, or made keepers of his country places: if they behaved ill, he dismissed them without hope of return.' In his promotions, nay almost in his benefits, you would have said there was a certain impartiality. 'The official person who had, by Abbot Hugo's order, put the fetters

Paltenerius. A proud, hard man.

on him at his return from Italy, was now supported
with food and clothes to the end of his days at Abbot
Samson's expense.'

Yet he did not forget benefits; far the reverse, when
an opportunity occurred of paying them at his own cost.
How pay them at the public cost—how, above all, by
setting fire to the public, as we said; clapping 'con-
flagrations' on the public, which the services of blockheads, *non-idonei*, intrinsically are! He was right
willing to remember friends, when it could be done.
Take these instances: 'A certain chaplain who had
maintained him at the Schools of Paris by the sale of
holy water, *quæstu aquæ benedictæ*—to this good chaplain he did give a vicarage, adequate to the comfortable
sustenance of him.' 'The Son of Elias too, that is, of
old Abbot Hugo's Cup-bearer, coming to do homage
for his Father's land, our Lord Abbot said to him in
full Court: "I have, for these seven years, put off taking
thy homage for the land which Abbot Hugo gave thy
Father, because that gift was to the damage of Elmswell, and a questionable one: but now I must profess
myself overcome; mindful of the kindness thy Father
did me when I was in bonds; because he sent me a cup
of the very wine his master had been drinking, and
bade me be comforted in God."'

'To Magister Walter, son of Magister William de Dice,
who wanted the vicarage of Chevington, he answered:
"Thy Father was Master of the Schools; and when I was
an indigent *clericus*, he granted me freely and in charity
an entrance to his School, and opportunity of learning;
wherefore I now, for the sake of God, grant to thee what

thou askest." ' Or lastly, take this good instance—and
a glimpse along with it, into long-obsolete times: 'Two
Milites of Risby, Willelm and Norman, being adjudged
in Court to come under his mercy, *in misericordia ejus'*,
for a certain very considerable fine of twenty shillings,
'he thus addressed them publicly on the spot: "When
I was a Cloister-monk, I was once sent to Durham on
business of our Church; and coming home again, the
dark night caught me at Risby, and I had to beg a
lodging there. I went to Dominus Norman's, and he
gave me a flat refusal. Going then to Dominus Willelm's,
and begging hospitality, I was by him honourably
received. The twenty shillings therefore of *mercy*, I,
without mercy, will exact from Dominus Norman; to
Dominus Willelm, on the other hand, I, with thanks,
will wholly remit the said sum." ' Men know not
always to whom they refuse lodgings; men have lodged
Angels unawares!

It is clear Abbot Samson had a talent; he had learned
to judge better than Lawyers, to manage better than
bred Bailiffs—a talent shining out indisputable, on whatever side you took him. 'An eloquent man he was,'
says Jocelin, 'both in French and Latin; but intent
more on the substance and method of what was to be
said, than on the ornamental way of saying it. He
could read English Manuscripts very elegantly, *elegan-
tissime*: he was wont to preach to the people in the
English tongue, though according to the dialect of
Norfolk, where he had been brought up; wherefore
indeed he had caused a Pulpit to be erected in our

Church both for ornament of the same, and for
the use of his audiences.' There preached he, according to the dialect of Norfolk; a man worth
going to hear.

That he was a just clear-hearted man, this, as the
basis of all true talent, is presupposed. How can a man,
without clear vision in his heart first of all, have any
clear vision in the head? It is impossible! Abbot
Samson was one of the justest of judges; insisted on
understanding the case to the bottom, and then swiftly
decided without feud or favour. For which reason,
indeed, the Dominus Rex, searching for such men, as
for hidden treasure and healing to his distressed realm,
had made him one of the new Itinerant Judges—such
as continue to this day. 'My curse on that Abbot's
court,' a suitor was heard imprecating, '*Maledicta sit
curia istius Abbatis*, where neither gold nor silver can
help me to confound my enemy!' And old friendships
and all connections forgotten, when you go to seek an
office from him! 'A kinless loon,' as the Scotch said
of Cromwell's new judges—intent on mere indifferent
fair-play!

Eloquence in three languages is good; but it is not
the best. To us, as already hinted, the Lord Abbot's
eloquence is less admirable than his *in*eloquence, his
great invaluable 'talent of silence'! ' "*Deus, Deus*,"
said the Lord Abbot to me once, when he heard the
Convent were murmuring at some act of his, "I have

The new Itinerant Judges. Judges on circuit appointed by
Henry II.
A kinless loon. A man that on the bench knew no kin.

much need to remember that Dream they had of me, that I was to rage among them like a wolf. Above all earthly things I dread their driving me to do it. How much do I hold in, and wink at; raging and shuddering in my own secret mind, and not outwardly at all!" He would boast to me at other times: "This and that I have seen, this and that I have heard; yet patiently stood it." He had this way, too, which I have never seen in any other man, that he affectionately loved many persons to whom he never or hardly ever showed a countenance of love. Once on my venturing to expostulate with him on the subject, he reminded me of Solomon: "Many sons I have; it is not fit that I should smile on them." He would suffer faults, damage from his servants, and know what he suffered, and not speak of it; but I think the reason was, he waited a good time for speaking of it, and in a wise way amending it. He intimated, openly in chapter to us all, that he would have no eavesdropping: "Let none," said he, "come to me secretly accusing another, unless he will publicly stand to the same; if he come otherwise, I will openly proclaim the name of him. I wish, too, that every Monk of you have free access to me, to speak of your needs or grievances when you will." '

The kinds of people Abbot Samson liked worst were these three: ' *Mendaces, ebriosi, verbosi,* Liars, drunkards, and wordy or windy persons '—not good kinds, any of them! He also much condemned 'persons given to murmur at their meat or drink, especially Monks of that disposition'. We remark, from the very first, his strict anxious order to his servants to provide handsomely for hospitality, to guard 'above all things that there be no shabbiness in the matter of meat and drink; no look of mean parsimony, *in novitate meâ*, at the beginning of my Abbotship'; and to the last he maintains a due opulence of table and equipment for others; but he is himself in the highest degree indifferent to all such things.

'Sweet milk, honey, and other naturally sweet kinds of food, were what he preferred to eat: but he had this virtue,' says Jocelin, 'he never changed the dish (*ferculum*) you set before him, be what it might. Once when I, still a novice, happened to be waiting table in the refectory, it came into my head' (rogue that I was!) 'to try if this were true; and I thought I would place before him a *ferculum* that would have displeased any other person, the very platter being black and broken. But he, seeing it, was as one that saw it not: and now some little delay taking place, my heart smote me that I had done this; and so, snatching up the platter (*discus*), I changed both it and its contents for a better, and put down that instead; which emendation he was angry at, and rebuked me for'—the stoical monastic man! 'For the first seven years he had commonly four sorts of dishes on his table; afterwards only three, except it might be presents, or venison from his own parks, or fishes from his ponds. And if, at any time, he had guests living in his house at the request of some great person, or of some friend, or had public messengers, or had harpers (*citharœdos*), or any one of that sort, he took the first opportunity of shifting to another of his Manor-houses, and so got rid of such superfluous individuals'—very prudently, I think.

As to his parks, in the general repair of buildings, general improvement and adornment of the St. Edmund Domains, 'he had laid out several, and stocked them with animals, retaining a proper huntsman with hounds: and, if any guest of great quality were there, our Lord Abbot with his Monks would sit in some opening of the woods, and see the dogs run; but he himself never meddled with hunting, that I saw'.

'In an opening of the woods'—for the country was still dark with wood in those days; and Scotland itself still rustled shaggy and leafy, like a damp black American Forest, with cleared spots and spaces here and there. Dryasdust advances several absurd hypotheses as to the insensible but almost total disappearance of these woods; the thick wreck of which now lies as *peat*, sometimes with huge heart-of-oak timber-logs embedded in it, on many a height and hollow. The simplest reason doubtless is, that by increase of husbandry, there was increase of cattle; increase of hunger for green spring food; and so, more and more, the new seedlings got yearly eaten out in April; and the old trees, having only a certain length of life in them, died gradually, no man heeding it, and disappeared into *peat*.

A sorrowful waste of noble wood and umbrage! Yes —but a very common one; the course of most things in this world. Monachism itself, so rich and fruitful once, is now all rotted into *peat*; lies sleek and buried—and a most feeble bog-grass of Dilettantism all the crop we reap from it! That also was frightful waste; perhaps among the saddest our England ever saw. Why will men destroy noble Forests, even when in part a nuisance, in such reckless manner; turning loose four-footed cattle and Henry-the-Eighths into them! The fifth part of our English soil, Dryasdust computes, lay consecrated to 'spiritual uses', better or worse; solemnly set apart to foster spiritual growth and culture of the soul, by the methods then known: and now—it too, like the four-fifths, fosters what? Gentle shepherd, tell me what!

CHAPTER XII

THE ABBOT'S TROUBLES

THE troubles of Abbot Samson, as he went along in this abstemious, reticent, rigorous way, were more than tongue can tell. The Abbot's mitre once set on his head, he knew rest no more. Double, double toil and trouble; that is the life of all governors that really govern: not the spoil of victory, only the glorious toil of battle can be theirs. Abbot Samson found all men more or less headstrong, irrational, prone to disorder; continually threatening to prove *un*governable.

His lazy Monks gave him most trouble. 'My heart is tortured,' said he, 'till we get out of debt, *cor meum cruciatum est.*' Your heart, indeed—but not altogether ours! By no devisable method, or none of three or four that he devised, could Abbot Samson get these Monks of his to keep their accounts straight; but always, do as he might, the Cellerarius at the end of the term is in a coil, in a flat deficit—verging again towards debt and Jews. The Lord Abbot at last declares sternly he will keep our accounts too himself; will appoint an officer of his own to see our Cellerarius keep them. Murmurs thereupon among us: Was the like ever heard? Our Cellerarius a cipher; the very Townsfolk know it: *subsannatio et derisio sumus*, we have become a laughing-stock to mankind. The Norfolk barrator and paltener!

Double, double toil and trouble. From the Witches' incantation in *Macbeth*, Act IV sc. i.

Paltener. Anglicized from *paltenerius* (see p. 79).

And consider, if the Abbot found such difficulty in the mere economic department, how much in more complex ones, in spiritual ones perhaps! He wears a stern calm face; raging and gnashing teeth, *fremens* and *frendens*, many times, in the secret of his mind. Withal, however, there is a noble slow perseverance in him; a strength of 'subdued rage' calculated to subdue most things: always, in the long-run, he contrives to gain his point.

Murmurs from the Monks, meanwhile, cannot fail; ever deeper murmurs, new grudges accumulating. At one time, on slight cause, some drop making the cup run over, they burst into open mutiny: the Cellarer will not obey, prefers arrest on bread-and-water to obeying; the Monks thereupon strike work; refuse to do the regular chanting of the day, at least the younger part of them with loud clamour and uproar refuse: Abbot Samson has withdrawn to another residence, acting only by messengers: the awful report circulates through St. Edmundsbury that the Abbot is in danger of being murdered by the Monks with their knives! How wilt thou appease this, Abbot Samson! Return; for the Monastery seems near catching fire!

Abbot Samson returns; sits in his *Talamus*, or inner room, hurls out a bolt or two of excommunication: lo, one disobedient Monk sits in limbo, excommunicated, with foot-shackles on him, all day; and three more our Abbot has gyved 'with the lesser sentence, to strike fear into the others'! Let the others think with whom they have to do. The others think; and fear enters

Talamus. See p. 36.

into them. 'On the morrow morning we decide on humbling ourselves before the Abbot, by word and gesture, in order to mitigate his mind. And so accordingly was done. He, on the other side, replying with much humility, yet always alleging his own justice and turning the blame on us, when he saw that we were conquered, became himself conquered. And bursting into tears, *perfusus lachrymis*, he swore that he had never grieved so much for anything in the world as for this, first on his own account, and then secondly and chiefly for the public scandal which had gone abroad, that St. Edmund's Monks were going to kill their Abbot. And when he had narrated how he went away on purpose till his anger should cool, repeating this word of the philosopher: "I would have taken vengeance on thee, had not I been angry," he arose weeping, and embraced each and all of us with the kiss of peace. He wept; we all wept'—what a picture! Behave better, ye remiss Monks, and thank Heaven for such an Abbot; or know at least that ye must and shall obey him.

Worn down in this manner, with incessant toil and tribulation, Abbot Samson had a sore time of it; his grizzled hair and beard grew daily greyer. Those Jews, in the first four years, had 'visibly emaciated him': Time, Jews, and the task of Governing, will make a man's beard very grey! 'In twelve years,' says Jocelin, 'our Lord Abbot had grown wholly white as snow, *totus efficitur albus sicut nix*.' White atop, like the granite mountains:—but his clear-beaming eyes still look out, in their stern clearness, in their sorrow and pity; the heart within him remains unconquered.

Nay sometimes there are gleams of hilarity too; little
snatches of encouragement granted even to a Governor.
'Once my Lord Abbot and I, coming down from London
through the Forest, I inquired of an old woman whom
we came up to, Whose wood this was, and of what manor;
who the master, who the keeper?' All this I knew very
well beforehand, and my Lord Abbot too, Bozzy that I
was! But 'the old woman answered, The wood belonged
to the new Abbot of St. Edmund's, was of the manor of
Harlow, and the keeper of it was one Arnald. How did
he behave to the people of the manor? I asked farther.
She answered that he used to be a devil incarnate, *dæmon
vivus*, an enemy of God, and flayer of the peasants' skins'
—skinning them like live eels, as the manner of some is:
'but that now he dreads the new Abbot, knowing him to
be a wise and sharp man, and so treats the people
reasonably, *tractat homines pacifice*'. Whereat the Lord
Abbot *factus est hilaris*—could not but take a triumphant
laugh for himself; and determines to leave that Harlow
manor yet unmeddled with, for a while.

A brave man, strenuously fighting, fails not of a little
triumph now and then, to keep him in heart. Everywhere we try at least to give the adversary as good as
he brings; and, with swift force or slow watchful
manœuvre, extinguish this and the other solecism, leave
one solecism less in God's Creation; and so *proceed*
with our battle, not slacken or surrender it! The Fifty
feudal Knights, for example, were of unjust greedy

Solecism. Literally, an impropriety in the use of language;
hence a breach of good manners; here used still more generally
for a wrong.

temper, and cheated us, in the Installation-day, of ten knights'-fees—but they know now whether that has profited them aught, and I Jocelin know. Our Lord Abbot for the moment had to endure it, and say nothing; but he watched his time.

Look also how my Lord of Clare, coming to claim his *un*due 'debt' in the Court of Witham, with barons and apparatus, gets a Roland for his Oliver! Jocelin shall report: 'The Earl, crowded round (*constipatus*) with many barons and men-at-arms, Earl Alberic and others standing by him, said: "That his bailiffs had given him to understand they were wont annually to receive for his behoof, from the Hundred of Risebridge and the bailiffs thereof, a sum of five shillings, which sum was now unjustly held back"; and he alleged farther that his predecessors had been infeft, at the Conquest, in the lands of Alfric son of Wisgar, who was Lord of that Hundred, as may be read in Doomsday Book by all persons. The Abbot, reflecting for a moment, without stirring from his place, made answer: "A wonderful deficit, my Lord Earl, this that thou mentionest! King Edward gave to St. Edmund that entire Hundred, and confirmed the same with his Charter; nor is there any mention there of those five shillings. It will behove thee to say, for what service, or on what ground, thou exactest those five shillings." Whereupon the Earl, consulting with his followers, replied: That he had to

A Roland for his Oliver. Tit for tat; alluding to Charlemagne's two knights, who fought each other for five days, with no advantage to either side.

Infeft. More commonly *enfeoffed*, invested with or granted the *fief* (fee, or feudal tenure) of an estate.

carry the Banner of St. Edmund in war-time, and for this duty the five shillings were his. To which the Abbot: "Certainly, it seems inglorious, if so great a man, Earl of Clare no less, receive so small a gift for such a service. To the Abbot of St. Edmund's it is no unbearable burden to give five shillings. But Roger Earl Bigot holds himself duly seised, and asserts that he by such seisin has the office of carrying St. Edmund's Banner; and he did carry it when the Earl of Leicester and his Flemings were beaten at Fornham. Then again Thomas de Mendham says that the right is his. When you have made out with one another, that this right is thine, come then and claim the five shillings, and I will promptly pay them!" Whereupon the Earl said, He would speak with Earl Roger his relative; and so the matter *cepit dilationem*,' and lies undecided to the end of the world. Abbot Samson answers by word or act, in this or the like pregnant manner, having justice on his side, innumerable persons: Pope's Legates, King's Viscounts, Canterbury Archbishops, Cellarers, *Sochemanni*—and leaves many a solecism extinguished.

On the whole, however, it is and remains sore work. 'One time, during my chaplaincy, I ventured to say to him: "*Domine*, I heard thee, this night after matins, wakeful, and sighing deeply, *valde suspirantem*, contrary to thy usual wont." He answered: "No wonder. Thou, son Jocelin, sharest in my good things, in food and drink, in riding and suchlike; but thou little thinkest concerning the management of House and Family, the various and arduous businesses of the Pastoral Care,

Seised ... seisin. 'In possession ... right of possession'.

which harass me, and make my soul to sigh and be anxious.' Whereto I, lifting up my hands to Heaven: "From such anxiety, Omnipotent merciful Lord deliver me!" I have heard the Abbot say, If he had been as he was before he became a Monk, and could have anywhere got five or six marcs of income,' some three-pound ten of yearly revenue, 'whereby to support himself in the schools, he would never have been Monk nor Abbot. Another time he said with an oath, If he had known what a business it was to govern the Abbey, he would rather have been Almoner, how much rather Keeper of the Books, than Abbot and Lord. That latter office he said he had always longed for, beyond any other. *Quis talia crederet?*' concludes Jocelin, 'Who can believe such things?'

Three-pound ten, and a life of Literature, especially of quiet Literature, without copyright, or world-celebrity of literary-gazettes—yes, thou brave Abbot Samson, for thyself it had been better, easier, perhaps also nobler! But then, for thy disobedient Monks, unjust Viscounts; for a Domain of St. Edmund overgrown with Solecisms, human and other, it had not been so well. Nay neither could *thy* Literature, never so quiet, have been easy. Literature, when noble, is not easy; but only when ignoble. Literature too is a quarrel, and internecine duel, with the whole World of Darkness that lies without one and within one—rather a hard fight at times, even with the three-pound ten secure. Thou, there where thou art, wrestle, and duel along, cheerfully to the end; and make no remarks!

CHAPTER XIII

IN PARLIAMENT

OF Abbot Samson's public business we say little, though
that also was great. He had to judge the people as
Justice Errant, to decide in weighty arbitrations and
public controversies; to equip his *milites*, send them duly
in war-time to the King—strive every way that the
Commonweal, in his quarter of it, take no damage.

Once, in the confused days of Lackland's usurpation,
while Cœur-de-Lion was away, our brave Abbot took
helmet himself, having first excommunicated all that
should favour Lackland; and led his men in person to
the siege of *Windleshora*, what we now call Windsor;
where Lackland had entrenched himself, the centre of
infinite confusions; some Reform Bill, then as now, being
greatly needed. There did Abbot Samson 'fight the
battle of reform'—with other ammunition, one hopes,
than 'tremendous cheering' and suchlike! For these
things he was called 'the magnanimous Abbot'.

He also attended duly in his place in Parliament *de
arduis regni*; attended especially, as in *arduissimo*, when
'the news reached London that King Richard was a
captive in Germany'. Here 'while all the barons sat to

De arduis regni. Concerning the difficulties of the kingdom.
Arduissimo. The most urgent difficulty.
King Richard was a captive in Germany. On his return from
the Crusade, in 1193.

consult,' and many of them looked blank enough, 'the Abbot started forth, *prosiliit coram omnibus*, in his place in Parliament, and said, That *he* was ready to go and seek his Lord the King, either clandestinely by subterfuge (*in tapinagio*), or by any other method; and search till he found him, and got certain notice of him; he for one! By which word,' says Jocelin, 'he acquired great praise for himself'—unfeigned commendation from the Able Editors of that age.

By which word—and also by which *deed*: for the Abbot actually went 'with rich gifts to the King in Germany'; Usurper Lackland being first rooted out from Windsor, and the King's peace somewhat settled.

As to these 'rich gifts', however, we have to note one thing: In all England, as appeared to the Collective Wisdom, there was not like to be treasure enough for ransoming King Richard; in which extremity certain Lords of the Treasury, *Justiciarii ad Scaccarium*, suggested that St. Edmund's Shrine, covered with thick gold, was still untouched. Could not it, in this extremity, be peeled off, at least in part; under condition, of course, of its being replaced when times mended? The Abbot, starting plumb up, *se erigens*, answered: 'Know ye for certain, that I will in nowise do this thing; nor is there any man who could force me to consent thereto. But I will open the doors of the Church: Let him that likes enter; let him that dares come forward!' Emphatic words, which created a sensation round the woolsack. For the Justiciaries of the *Scaccarium* answered, 'with oaths, each for himself: "I won't come forward, for my share; nor will I, nor I! The distant and absent who offended him, Saint Edmund has been known to punish fearfully; much more will he those close by, who lay violent hands on his coat, and would strip it off!" These things being said, the Shrine was not meddled with, nor any ransom levied for it.'

For Lords of the Treasury have in all times their impassable limits, be it by 'force of public opinion' or otherwise; and in those days a heavenly Awe over-shadowed and encompassed, as it still ought and must, all earthly Business whatsoever.

CHAPTER XIV

HENRY OF ESSEX

OF St. Edmund's fearful avengements have they not the remarkable instance still before their eyes? He that will go to Reading Monastery may find there, now tonsured into a mournful penitent Monk, the once proud Henry Earl of Essex; and discern how St. Edmund punishes terribly, yet with mercy! This Narrative is too significant to be omitted as a document of the Time. Our Lord Abbot, once on a visit at Reading, heard the particulars from Henry's own mouth; and thereupon charged one of his monks to write it down—as accordingly the Monk has done, in ambitious rhetorical Latin; inserting the same, as episode, among Jocelin's garrulous leaves. Read it here; with ancient yet with modern eyes.

Henry Earl of Essex, standard-bearer of England, had high places and emoluments; had a haughty high soul, yet with various flaws, or rather with one many-branched flaw and crack, running through the texture of it. For example, did he not treat Gilbert de Cereville in the most shocking manner? He cast Gilbert into prison; and, with chains and slow torments, wore the life out of him there. And Gilbert's crime was understood to be only that of innocent Joseph: the Lady Essex was a Potiphar's Wife, and had accused poor Gilbert! Other cracks, and

D

branches of that widespread flaw in the Standard-
bearer's soul we could point out: but indeed the main
stem and trunk of all is too visible in this, That he had
no right reverence for the Heavenly in Man—that far
from showing due reverence to St. Edmund, he did not
even show him common justice. While others in the
Eastern Counties were adorning and enlarging with rich
gifts St. Edmund's resting-place, which had become a
city of refuge for many things, this Earl of Essex flatly
defrauded him, by violence or quirk of law, of five
shillings yearly, and converted said sum to his own poor
uses! Nay, in another case of litigation, the unjust
Standard-bearer, for his own profit, asserting that the
cause belonged not to St. Edmund's Court, but to *his*
in Lailand Hundred, 'involved us in travellings and
innumerable expenses, vexing the servants of St.
Edmund for a long tract of time'. In short, he is
without reverence for the Heavenly, this Standard-
bearer; reveres only the Earthly, Gold-coined; and has
a most morbid lamentable flaw in the texture of him.
It cannot come to good.

Accordingly, the same flaw, or St.-Vitus' *tic*, manifests
itself ere long in another way. In the year 1157, he
went with his Standard to attend King Henry, our
blessed Sovereign (whom *we* saw afterwards at Waltham), in his War with the Welsh. A somewhat disastrous War; in which while King Henry and his force
were struggling to retreat Parthian-like, endless clouds
of exasperated Welshmen hemming them in, and now
we had come to the 'difficult pass of Coleshill', and as

St.-Vitus' tic. Facial neuralgia, similar to St. Vitus's Dance.

it were to the nick of destruction—Henry Earl of Essex
shrieks out on a sudden (blinded doubtless by his inner
flaw, or 'evil genius' as some name it), That King Henry
is killed, That all is lost—and flings down his Standard
to shift for itself there! And, certainly enough, all *had*
been lost, had all men been as he—had not brave men,
without such miserable jerking *tic-douloureux* in the
souls of them, come dashing up, with blazing swords,
and looks, and asserted, That nothing was lost yet, that
all must be regained yet. In this manner King Henry
and his force got safely retreated, Parthian-like, from
the pass of Coleshill and the Welsh War. But, once
home again, Earl Robert de Montfort, a kinsman of this
Standard-bearer's, rises up in the King's Assembly to
declare openly that such a man is unfit for bearing
English Standards, being in fact either a special traitor,
or something almost worse, a coward namely, or universal
traitor. Wager of Battle in consequence; solemn Duel,
by the King's appointment, 'in a certain Island of the
Thames-stream at Reading, *apud Radingas*, short way
from the Abbey there'. King, Peers, and an immense
multitude of people, on such scaffoldings and heights as
they can come at, are gathered round, to see what issue
the business will take. The business takes this bad
issue, in our Monk's own words faithfully rendered:

'And it came to pass, while Robert de Montfort
thundered on him manfully (*viriliter intonâsset*) with
hard and frequent strokes, and a valiant beginning

Parthian-like. Adopting the tactics of the ancient Parthians,
aiming their shafts while avoiding or retreating from their foes;
hence the expression, 'a Parthian shot'.

promised the fruit of victory, Henry of Essex, rather
giving way, glanced round on all sides; and lo, at the
rim of the horizon, on the confines of the River and
land, he discerned the glorious King and Martyr Edmund,
in shining armour, and as if hovering in the air; looking
towards him with severe countenance, nodding his head
with a mien and motion of austere anger. At St.
Edmund's hand there stood also another Knight, Gilbert
de Cereville, whose armour was not so splendid, whose
stature was less gigantic; casting vengeful looks at him.
This he seeing with his eyes, remembered that old crime
brings new shame. And now wholly desperate, and
changing reason into violence, he took the part of one
blindly attacking, not skilfully defending. Who while
he struck fiercely was more fiercely struck; and so, in
short, fell down vanquished, and it was thought slain.
As he lay there for dead, his kinsmen, Magnates of
England, besought the King, that the Monks of Reading
might have leave to bury him. However, he proved
not to be dead, but got well again among them; and
now, with recovered health, assuming the Regular
Habit, he strove to wipe out the stain of his former
life, to cleanse the long week of his dissolute history by
at least a purifying sabbath, and cultivate the studies
of Virtue into fruits of eternal Felicity.'

Thus does the Conscience of man project itself athwart
whatsoever of knowledge or surmise, of imagination,

Regular Habit. The dress of a monk, who belonged to one of
the *regular* Orders of the Church, as distinguished from the
ordinary or secular priests.

understanding, faculty, acquirement, or natural disposition, he has in him; and, like light through coloured glass, paint strange pictures 'on the rim of the horizon' and elsewhere! Truly, this same 'sense of the Infinite nature of Duty' is the central part of all with us; a ray as of Eternity and Immortality, immured in dusky many-coloured Time, and its deaths and births. Your 'coloured glass' varies so much from century to century —and, in certain money-making, game-preserving centuries, it gets so terribly opaque! Not a Heaven with cherubim surrounds you then, but a kind of vacant leaden-coloured Hell. One day it will again cease to be *opaque*, this 'coloured glass'. Nay, may it not become at once translucent and *un*coloured? Painting no Pictures more for us, but only the everlasting Azure itself? That will be a right glorious consummation!

Saint Edmund from the horizon's edge, in shining armour, threatening the misdoer in his hour of extreme need: it is beautiful, it is great and true. So old, yet so modern, actual; true yet for every one of us, as for Henry the Earl and Monk! A glimpse as of the Deepest in Man's Destiny, which is the same for all times and ages. Yes, Henry my brother, there in thy extreme need, thy soul is *lamed*; and behold thou canst not so much as fight! For Justice and Reverence *are* the everlasting central Law of this Universe; and to forget them, and have all the Universe against one, God and one's own Self for enemies, and only the Devil and the Dragons for friends, is not that a 'lameness' like few? That some shining armed St. Edmund hang minatory on thy horizon, that infinite sulphur-lakes hang minatory,

or do not now hang—this alters no whit the eternal
fact of the thing. I say, thy soul is lamed, and the
God and all Godlike in it marred: lamed, paralytic,
tending towards baleful eternal death, whether thou
know it or not—nay hadst thou never known it, that
surely had been worst of all!

Thus, at any rate, by the heavenly Awe that over-
shadows earthly Business, does Samson, readily in those
days, save St. Edmund's Shrine, and innumerable still
more precious things.

CHAPTER XV

PRACTICAL-DEVOTIONAL

HERE indeed, by rule of antagonisms, may be the place to mention that, after King Richard's return, there was a liberty of tourneying given to the fighting-men of England: that a Tournament was proclaimed in the Abbot's domain, 'between Thetford and St. Edmundsbury'—perhaps in the Euston region, on Fakenham Heights, midway between these two localities: that it was publicly prohibited by our Lord Abbot; and nevertheless was held in spite of him—and by the parties, as would seem, considered 'a gentle and free passage of arms'.

Nay, next year, there came to the same spot four-and-twenty young men, sons of Nobles, for another passage of arms; who, having completed the same, all rode into St. Edmundsbury to lodge for the night. Here is modesty! Our Lord Abbot, being instructed of it, ordered the Gates to be closed; the whole party shut in. The morrow was the Vigil of the Apostles Peter and Paul; no outgate on the morrow. Giving their promise not to depart without permission, those four-and-twenty young bloods dieted all that day (*manducaverunt*) with the Lord Abbot, waiting for trial on the morrow. 'But after dinner'—mark it, posterity!—'the Lord Abbot retiring into his *Talamus*, they all started up, and began carolling and singing (*carolare et cantare*); sending into the Town for wine; drinking, and afterwards howling (*ululantes*)—totally depriving the Abbot and Convent of their afternoon's nap; doing all this in derision of the Lord Abbot, and spending in such fashion the whole day till evening, nor would they desist at the Lord Abbot's order! Night coming on, they broke the bolts of the Town-Gates, and went off by violence!' Was the like ever heard of? The roysterous young dogs; carolling, howling, breaking the Lord Abbot's sleep—after that sinful chivalry cockfight of theirs! They too are a feature of distant centuries, as of near ones. St. Edmund on the edge of your horizon, or whatever else there, young scamps, in the dandy state, whether cased in iron or in whalebone, begin to caper and carol on the green Earth! Our Lord Abbot excommunicated most of them; and they gradually came in for repentance.

Excommunication is a great recipe with our Lord Abbot; the prevailing purifier in those ages. Thus when the Townsfolk and Monks' menials quarrelled once at the Christmas Mysteries in St. Edmund's Churchyard, and 'from words it came to cuffs, and from cuffs to cutting and the effusion of blood'—our Lord Abbot excommunicates sixty of the rioters, with bell, book, and candle (*accensis candelis*), at one stroke. Whereupon they all come suppliant, indeed nearly naked, 'nothing on but their breeches, *omnino nudi præter femoralia*, and prostrate themselves at the Church-door'. Figure that!

In fact, by excommunication or persuasion, by impetuosity of driving or adroitness in leading, this Abbot, it is now becoming plain everywhere, is a man that generally remains master at last. He tempers his medicine to the malady, now hot, now cool; prudent though fiery, an eminently practical man. Nay sometimes in his adroit practice there are swift turns almost of a surprising nature! Once, for example, it chanced that Geoffrey Riddell Bishop of Ely, a Prelate rather troublesome to our Abbot, made a request of him for timber from his woods towards certain edifices going on at Glemsford. The Abbot, a great builder himself, disliked the request; could not, however, give it a negative. While he lay, therefore, at his Manor-house of Melford not long after, there comes to him one of the Lord Bishop's men or monks, with a message from his Lordship: 'That he now begged permission to cut down the requisite trees in Elmswell Wood'—so said the monk: Elms*well*, where there are no trees but scrubs and shrubs, instead of Elm*set*, our true *nemus* and high-towering oak-wood, here on Melford Manor! Elmswell? The Lord Abbot, in surprise, inquires privily of Richard his Forester; Richard answers that my Lord of Ely has already had his *carpentarii* in Elm*set*, and marked out for his own use all the best trees in the compass of it. Abbot Samson thereupon answers the monk: 'Elmswell? Yes surely, be it as my Lord Bishop wishes.' The successful monk, on the morrow morning, hastens home to Ely; but, on the morrow morning, 'directly after mass', Abbot Samson too was busy! The successful monk, arriving at Ely, is rated for a goose and an owl; is ordered back to say that Elmset

Nemus. A grove.

* D

was the place meant. Alas, on arriving at Elmset, he
finds the Bishop's trees, they 'and a hundred more',
all felled and piled, and the stamp of St. Edmund's
Monastery burnt into them—for roofing of the great
tower we are building there! Your importunate Bishop
must seek wood for Glemsford edifices in some other
nemus than this. A practical Abbot!

We said withal there was a terrible flash of anger in
him; witness his address to old Herbert the Dean, who
in a too thrifty manner has erected a windmill for himself on his glebe-lands at Haberdon. On the morrow,
after mass, our Lord Abbot orders the Cellerarius to
send off his carpenters to demolish the said structure
brevi manu, and lay up the wood in safe keeping. Old
Dean Herbert, hearing what was toward, comes totter-
ing along hither, to plead humbly for himself and his
mill. The Abbot answers: 'I am obliged to thee as if
thou hadst cut off both my feet! By God's face, *per
os Dei*, I will not eat bread till that fabric be torn in
pieces. Thou art an old man, and shouldst have known
that neither the King nor his Justiciary dare change
aught within the Liberties without consent of Abbot
and Convent: and thou hast presumed on such a thing?
I tell thee, it will *not* be without damage to my mills;
for the Townsfolk will go to thy mill, and grind their
corn (*bladum suum*) at their own good pleasure; nor can
I hinder them, since they are free men. I will allow
no new mills on such principle. Away, away; before
thou gettest home again, thou shalt see what thy mill

Brevi manu. At once.
Liberties. The districts over which the abbot had exclusive rights.

has grown to!' The very reverend the old Dean totters
home again, in all haste; tears the mill in pieces by his
own *carpentarii*, to save at least the timber; and Abbot
Samson's workmen, coming up, find the ground already
clear of it.

Easy to bully-down poor old rural Deans, and blow
their windmills away: but who is the man that dare
abide King Richard's anger; cross the Lion in his path,
and take him by the whiskers! Abbot Samson too; he
is that man, with justice on his side. The case was this.
Adam de Cokefield, one of the chief feudatories of St.
Edmund, and a principal man in the Eastern Counties,
died, leaving large possessions, and for heiress a daughter
of three months; who by clear law, as all men know,
became thus Abbot Samson's ward; whom accordingly
he proceeded to dispose of to such person as seemed
fittest. But now King Richard has another person in
view, to whom the little ward and her great possessions
were a suitable thing. He, by letter, requests that Abbot
Samson will have the goodness to give her to this person.
Abbot Samson, with deep humility, replies that she is
already given. New letters from Richard, of severer
tenor; answered with new deep humilities, with gifts
and entreaties, with no promise of obedience. King
Richard's ire is kindled; messengers arrive at St.
Edmundsbury, with emphatic message to obey or
tremble! Abbot Samson, wisely silent as to the King's
threats, makes answer: 'The King can send if he will,
and seize the ward: force and power he has to do his
pleasure, and abolish the whole Abbey. But I, for my

part, never can be bent to wish this that he seeks, nor
shall it by me be ever done. For there is danger lest
such things be made a precedent of, to the prejudice of my
successors. *Videat Altissimus*, Let the Most High look on
it. Whatsoever thing shall befall I will patiently endure.'

Such was Abbot Samson's deliberate decision. Why
not? Cœur-de-Lion is very dreadful, but not the
dreadfulest. *Videat Altissimus.* I reverence Cœur-de-
Lion to the marrow of my bones, and will in all right
things be *homo suus*; but it is not, properly speaking,
with terror, with any fear at all. On the whole, have
I not looked on the face of 'Satan with outspread
wings'; steadily into Hell-fire these seven-and-forty
years—and was not melted into terror even at that,
such the Lord's goodness to me? Cœur-de-Lion!

Richard swore tornado oaths, worse than our armies
in Flanders, To be revenged on that proud Priest. But
in the end he discovered that the Priest was right; and
forgave him, and even loved him. 'King Richard
wrote, soon after, to Abbot Samson, That he wanted
one or two of the St. Edmundsbury dogs, which he
heard were good'. Abbot Samson sent him dogs of the
best; Richard replied by the present of a ring, which
Pope Innocent the Third had given him. Thou brave
Richard, thou brave Samson! Richard too, I suppose,
'loved a man', and knew one when he saw him.

No one will accuse our Lord Abbot of wanting worldly

Homo suus. His liegeman.
Worse than our armies in Flanders. Alluding to Uncle Toby's
remark: 'Our armies swore terribly in Flanders, but nothing to
this' (Sterne's *Tristram Shandy*, III, xi).

wisdom, due interest in worldly things. A skilful man;
full of cunning insight, lively interests; always discerning
the road to his object, be it circuit, be it short-cut, and
victoriously travelling forward thereon. Nay rather it
might seem, from Jocelin's Narrative, as if he had his
eye all but exclusively directed on terrestrial matters,
and was much too secular for a devout man. But this
too, if we examine it, was right. For it is *in* the world
that a man, devout or other, has his life to lead, his work
waiting to be done. The basis of Abbot Samson's, we
shall discover, was truly religion, after all. Returning
from his dusty pilgrimage, with such welcome as we
saw, 'he sat down at the foot of St. Edmund's Shrine'.
Not a talking theory, that; no, a silent practice: Thou,
St. Edmund, with what lies in thee, thou now must
help me, or none will!

This also is a significant fact: the zealous interest our
Abbot took in the Crusades. To all noble Christian
hearts of that era, what earthly enterprise so noble?
'When Henry II, having taken the cross, came to St.
Edmund's, to pay his devotions before setting out, the
Abbot secretly made for himself a cross of linen cloth:
and, holding this in one hand and a threaded needle in
the other, asked 'leave of the King to assume it'. The
King could not spare Samson out of England—the King
himself indeed never went. But the Abbot's eye was
set on the Holy Sepulchre, as on the spot of this Earth
where the true cause of Heaven was deciding itself. 'At
the retaking of Jerusalem by the Pagans, Abbot Samson
put on a *cilice* and hair-shirt, and wore under-garments

Cilice. See note, p. 16.

of hair-cloth ever after; he abstained also from flesh
and flesh-meats (*carne et carneis*) thenceforth to the end
of his life.' Like a dark cloud eclipsing the hopes of
Christendom, those tidings cast their shadow over
St. Edmundsbury too: Shall Samson Abbas take
pleasure while Christ's Tomb is in the hands of the
Infidel? Samson, in pain of body, shall daily be
reminded of it, daily be admonished to grieve for it.

The great antique heart: how like a child's in its
simplicity, like a man's in its earnest solemnity and
depth! Heaven lies over him wheresoever he goes or
stands on the Earth; making all the Earth a mystic
Temple to him, the Earth's business all a kind of
worship. Glimpses of bright creatures flash in the
common sunlight; angels yet hover doing God's messages
among men: that rainbow was set in the clouds by the
hand of God! Wonder, miracle encompass the man;
he lives in an element of miracle; Heaven's splendour
over his head, Hell's darkness under his feet. A great
Law of Duty, high as these two Infinitudes, dwarfing
all else, annihilating all else—making royal Richard as
small as peasant Samson, smaller if need be! The
'imaginative faculties'? 'Rude poetic ages?' The
'primeval poetic element'? Oh, for God's sake, good
reader, talk no more of all that! It was not a Dilettantism this of Abbot Samson. It was a Reality, and
it is one. The garment only of it is dead; the essence
of it lives through all Time and all Eternity!

CHAPTER XVI

ST. EDMUND

ABBOT SAMSON built many useful, many pious edifices; human dwellings, churches, church-steeples, barns—all fallen now and vanished, but useful while they stood. He built and endowed 'the Hospital of Babwell'; built 'fit houses for the St. Edmundsbury Schools'. Many are the roofs once 'thatched with reeds' which he 'caused to be covered with tiles'; or if they were churches, probably 'with lead'. For all ruinous incomplete things, buildings or other, were an eye-sorrow to the man. We saw his 'great tower of St. Edmund's'; or at least the roof-timbers of it, lying cut and stamped in Elmset Wood. To change combustible decaying reed-thatch into tile or lead; and material, still more, moral wreck into rain-tight order, what a comfort to Samson!

One of the things he could not in any wise but rebuild was the great Altar, aloft on which stood the Shrine itself; the great Altar, which had been damaged by fire, by the careless rubbish and careless candle of two somnolent Monks, one night—the Shrine escaping almost as if by miracle! Abbot Samson read his Monks a severe lecture: 'A Dream one of us had, that he saw St. Edmund naked and in lamentable plight. Know ye the interpretation of that Dream? St. Edmund proclaims himself naked, because ye defraud the naked Poor of your old clothes, and give with reluctance what ye are bound to give them of meat and drink: the idleness moreover

and negligence of the Sacristan and his people is too
evident from the late misfortune by fire. Well might
our Holy Martyr seem to lie cast out from his Shrine,
and say with groans that he was stript of his garments,
and wasted with hunger and thirst!'

This is Abbot Samson's interpretation of the Dream
—diametrically the reverse of that given by the Monks
themselves, who scruple not to say privily: 'It is *we*
that are the naked and famished limbs of the Martyr;
we whom the Abbot curtails of all our privileges, setting
his own official to control our very Cellarer!' Abbot
Samson adds, that this judgment by fire has fallen upon
them for murmuring about their meat and drink.

Clearly enough, meanwhile, the Altar, whatever the
burning of it mean or foreshadow, must needs be re-
edified. Abbot Samson re-edifies it, all of polished
marble; with the highest stretch of art and sumptuosity,
re-embellishes the Shrine for which it is to serve as
pediment. Nay farther, as had ever been among his
prayers, he enjoys, he sinner, a glimpse of the glorious
Martyr's very Body in the process; having solemnly
opened the *Loculus*, Chest, or sacred Coffin, for that
purpose. It is the culminating moment of Abbot Samson's life. Bozzy Jocelin himself rises into a kind of
Psalmist solemnity on this occasion; the laziest monk
'weeps' warm tears, as *Te Deum* is sung.

Very strange—how far vanished from us in these
unworshipping ages of ours! The Patriot Hampden,

Hampden. An allusion to the disinterment, in 1828, at
Chalgrove churchyard, of John Hampden, the parliamentarian
hero, in order to ascertain the true cause of his death (in
1643).

best beatified man we have, had lain in like manner
some two centuries in his narrow home, when certain
dignitaries of us, 'and twelve grave-diggers with pulleys',
raised him also up, under cloud of night, cut off his
arm with penknives, pulled the scalp off his head—and
otherwise worshipped our Hero Saint in the most
amazing manner! Let the modern eye look earnestly
on that old midnight hour in St. Edmundsbury Church,
shining yet on us, ruddy-bright, through the depths of
seven hundred years; and consider mournfully what our
Hero-worship once was, and what it now is! We
translate with all the fidelity we can:

'The Festival of St. Edmund now approaching, the
marble blocks are polished, and all things are in readi-
ness for lifting of the Shrine to its new place. A fast
of three days was held by all the people, the cause and
meaning thereof being publicly set forth to them. The
Abbot announces to the Convent that all must prepare
themselves for transferring of the Shrine, and appoints
time and way for the work. Coming therefore that
night to matins, we found the great Shrine (*feretrum
magnum*) raised upon the Altar, but empty; covered all
over with white doeskin leather, fixed to the wood with
silver nails; but one pannel of the Shrine was left down
below, and resting thereon, beside its old column of the
Church, the Loculus with the Sacred Body yet lay where
it was wont. Praises being sung, we all proceeded to
commence our disciplines (*ad disciplinas suscipiendas*).
These finished, the Abbot and certain with him are
clothed in their albs; and, approaching reverently, set
about uncovering the Loculus. There was an outer

cloth of linen, enwrapping the Loculus and all; this we
found tied on the upper side with strings of its own:
within this was a cloth of silk, and then another linen
cloth, and then a third; and so at last the Loculus was
uncovered, and seen resting on a little tray of wood,
that the bottom of it might not be injured by the stone.
Over the breast of the Martyr, there lay, fixed to the
surface of the Loculus, a Golden Angel about the length
of a human foot; holding in one hand a golden sword,
and in the other a banner: under this there was a hole
in the lid of the Loculus, on which the ancient servants
of the Martyr had been wont to lay their hands for
touching the Sacred Body.   And over the figure of the
Angel was this verse inscribed:

> *'Martiris ecce zoma servat Michaelis agalma.*

At the head and foot of the Loculus were iron rings
whereby it could be lifted.

'Lifting the Loculus and Body, therefore, they carried
it to the Altar; and I put-to my sinful hand to help in
carrying, though the Abbot had commanded that none
should approach except called.   And the Loculus was
placed in the Shrine; and the pannel it had stood on was
put in its place, and the Shrine for the present closed.
We all thought that the Abbot would show the Loculus
to the people; and bring out the Sacred Body again, at
a certain period of the Festival.   But in this we were
woefully mistaken, as the sequel shows.

'For in the fourth holiday of the Festival, while the

Martiris ecce . . . 'Behold, Michael's image guards the
body of the Martyr.'

Convent were all singing *Completorium*, our Lord Abbot
spoke privily with the Sacristan and Walter the Medicus;
and order was taken that twelve of the Brethren should
be appointed against midnight, who were strong for
carrying the pannel-planks of the Shrine, and skilful in
unfixing them, and putting them together again. The
Abbot then said that it was among his prayers to look
once upon the Body of his Patron; and that he wished
the Sacristan and Walter the Medicus to be with him.
The Twelve appointed Brethren were these: The Abbot's
two Chaplains, the two Keepers of the Shrine, the two
Masters of the Vestry; and six more, namely, the
Sacristan Hugo, Walter the Medicus, Augustin, William
of Dice, Robert, and Richard. I, alas, was not of the
number.

'The Convent therefore being all asleep, these Twelve,
clothed in their albs, with the Abbot, assembled at the
Altar; and opening a pannel of the Shrine, they took
out the Loculus; laid it on a table, near where the
Shrine used to be; and made ready for unfastening the
lid, which was joined and fixed to the Loculus with
sixteen very long nails. Which when, with difficulty,
they had done, all except the two fore-named associates
are ordered to draw back. The Abbot and they two
were alone privileged to look in. The Loculus was so
filled with the Sacred Body that you could scarcely
put a needle between the head and the wood, or between
the feet and the wood: the head lay united to the body,
a little raised with a small pillow. But the Abbot,
looking close, found now a silk cloth veiling the whole

Completorium. Compline, the closing service of the day.

Body, and then a linen cloth of wondrous whiteness;
and upon the head was spread a small linen cloth, and
then another small and most fine silk cloth, as if it were
the veil of a nun. These coverings being lifted off,
they found now the Sacred Body all wrapt in linen; and
so at length the lineaments of the same appeared. But
here the Abbot stopped; saying he durst not proceed
farther, or look at the sacred flesh naked. Taking the
head between his hands, he thus spake, groaning:
"Glorious Martyr, holy Edmund, blessed be the hour
when thou wert born. Glorious Martyr, turn it not to
my perdition that I have so dared to touch thee, I
miserable and sinful; thou knowest my devout love, and
the intention of my mind." And proceeding, he touched
the eyes; and the nose, which was very massive and
prominent (*valde grossum et valde eminentem*); and then
he touched the breast and arms; and raising the left
arm he touched the fingers, and placed his own fingers
between the sacred fingers. And proceeding he found
the feet standing stiff up, like the feet of a man dead
yesterday; and he touched the toes and counted them
(*tangendo numeravit*).

'And now it was agreed that the other Brethren
should be called forward to see the miracles; and
accordingly those ten now advanced, and along with
them six others who had stolen in without the Abbot's
assent, namely, Walter of St. Alban's, Hugh the Infirmirarius, Gilbert brother of the Prior, Richard of
Henham, Jocellus our Cellarer, and Turstan the Little;
and all these saw the Sacred Body, but Turstan alone

Infirmirarius. Official who tended the sick.

of them put forth his hand, and touched the Saint's knees and feet. And that there might be abundance of witnesses, one of our Brethren, John of Dice, sitting on the roof of the Church, with the servants of the Vestry, and looking through, clearly saw all these things.'

What a scene; shining luminous effulgent, as the lamps of St. Edmund do, through the dark Night; John of Dice, with vestrymen, clambering on the roof to look through; the Convent all asleep, and the Earth all asleep—and since then, Seven Centuries of Time mostly gone to sleep! Yes, there, sure enough, is the martyred Body of Edmund, landlord of the Eastern Counties, who, nobly doing what he liked with his own, was slain three hundred years ago: and a noble awe surrounds the memory of him, symbol and promoter of many other right noble things.

But have not we now advanced to strange new stages of Hero-worship, now in the little Church of Hampden, with our penknives out, and twelve grave-diggers with pulleys? The manner of men's Hero-worship, verily it is the innermost fact of their existence, and determines all the rest—at public hustings, in private drawing-rooms, in church, in market, and wherever else. Have true reverence, and what indeed is inseparable there-from, reverence the right man, all is well; have sham-reverence, and what also follows, greet with it the wrong man, then all is ill, and there is nothing well. Alas, if Hero-worship become Dilettantism, and all except Mammonism be a vain grimace, how much, in this most earnest Earth, has gone and is evermore going to fatal destruction, and lies wasting in quiet lazy ruin, no man regarding it! Till at length no heavenly *Ism* any longer coming down upon us, *Isms* from the other quarter have to mount up. For the Earth, I say, is an earnest place; Life is no grimace, but a most serious fact. And so, under universal Dilettantism much having been stript bare, not the souls of men only, but their very bodies and bread-cupboards having been stript bare, and life now no longer possible—all is reduced to desperation, to the iron law of Necessity and very Fact again; and to temper Dilettantism, and astonish it, and burn it up with infernal fire, arises Chartism, *Bare-back-ism*, Sansculottism so-called! May the gods, and what of unworshipped heroes still remain among us, avert the omen!

But however this may be, St. Edmund's Loculus, we find, has the veils of silk and linen reverently replaced, the lid fastened down again with its sixteen ancient nails; is wrapt in a new costly covering of silk, the gift of Hubert Archbishop of Canterbury: and through the sky-window John of Dice sees it lifted to its place in the Shrine, the pannels of this latter duly refixed, fit parchment documents being introduced withal—and now John and his vestry-men can slide down from the roof, for all is over, and the Convent wholly awakens to matins. 'When we assembled to sing matins,' says Jocelin, 'and understood what had been done, grief

Sansculottism. Doctrine of the French revolutionaries, called *sansculottes* by the aristocrats; referring to the fact that the Revolutionaries adopted pantaloons in place of fashionable knee-breeches (*culottes*).

took hold of all that had not seen these things, each
saying to himself: "Alas, I was deceived." Matins
over, the Abbot called the Convent to the great Altar;
and briefly recounting the matter, alleged that it had
not been in his power, nor was it permissible or fit, to
invite us all to the sight of such things. At hearing of
which, we all wept, and with tears sang *Te Deum
laudamus*; and hastened to toll the bells in the Choir.'

Stupid blockheads, to reverence their St. Edmund's
dead Body in this manner? Yes, brother—and yet, on
the whole, who knows how to reverence the Body of a
Man? It is the most reverend phenomenon under this
Sun. For the Highest God dwells visible in that mystic
unfathomable Visibility, which calls itself 'I' on the
Earth. 'Bending before men', says Novalis, 'is a reverence done to this Revelation in the Flesh. We touch
Heaven when we lay our hand on a human Body.' And
the Body of one Dead—a temple where the Hero-soul
once was and now is not: Oh, all mystery, all pity, all
mute *awe* and wonder; *Super*naturalism brought home
to the very dullest; Eternity laid open, and the nether
Darkness and the upper Light-Kingdoms, do conjoin
there, or exist nowhere!

Abbot Samson, at this culminating point of his
existence, may, and indeed must, be left to vanish with
his Life-scenery from the eyes of modern men. He had
to run into France, to settle with King Richard for the
military service there of his St. Edmundsbury Knights;
and with great labour got it done. He had to decide

Novalis. Pen-name of the German mystic and poet, Friedrich
von Hardenburg (1772-1801).

on the dilapidated Coventry Monks; and with great labour, and much pleading and journeying, got them reinstated; dined with them all, and with the 'Masters of the Schools of Oxneford'—the veritable Oxford *Caput* sitting there at dinner, in a dim but undeniable manner, in the City of Peeping Tom! He had, not without labour, to controvert the intrusive Bishop of Ely, the intrusive Abbot of Cluny. Magnanimous Samson, his life is but a labour and a journey; a bustling and a justling, till the still Night come. He is sent for again, over sea, to advise King Richard touching certain Peers of England, who had taken the Cross, but never followed it to Palestine; whom the Pope is inquiring after. The magnanimous Abbot makes preparation for departure; departs, and—— And Jocelin's Boswellean Narrative, suddenly shorn through by the scissors of Destiny, *ends*. There are no words more; but a black line, and leaves of blank paper. Irremediable: the miraculous hand, that held all this theatric-machinery, suddenly quits hold; impenetrable Time-Curtains rush down; in the mind's eye all is again dark, void; with loud dinning in the mind's ear, our real-phantasmagory of St. Edmundsbury plunges into the bosom of the Twelfth Century again, and all is over. Monks, Abbot, Hero-worship, Government, Obedience, Cœur-de-Lion and St. Edmund's Shrine, vanish like Mirza's Vision; and there is nothing left but a mutilated black

City of Peeping Tom. Coventry, in allusion to the legend of the Lady Godiva.

Mirza's Vision. A well-known essay of Addison's is entitled *The Vision of Mirzah*, an allegory of human life.

Ruin amid green botanic expanses, and oxen, sheep,
and dilettanti pasturing in their places.

Not without a mournful interest have we surveyed
that authentic image of a Time now wholly swallowed.
Mournful reflections crowd on us—and yet consolatory.
How many brave men have lived before Agamemnon!
Here is a brave governor Samson, a man fearing God,
and fearing nothing else; of whom as First Lord of the
Treasury, as King, Chief Editor, High Priest, we could
be so glad and proud; of whom nevertheless Fame
has altogether forgotten to make mention! The faint
image of him, revived in this hour, is found in the
gossip of one poor Monk, and in Nature nowhere else.
Oblivion had so nigh swallowed him altogether, even to
the echo of his ever having existed.   What regiments
and hosts and generations of such has Oblivion already
swallowed!   Their crumbled dust makes up the soil our
life-fruit grows on.   Said I not, as my old Norse Fathers
taught me, The Life-tree Igdrasil, which waves round
thee in this hour, whereof thou in this hour art portion,
has its roots down deep in the oldest Death-Kingdoms;
and grows; the Three Nornas, or *Times*, Past, Present,
Future, watering it from the Sacred Well!
     The first man who, looking with opened soul on this
august Heaven and Earth, this Beautiful and Awful,
which we name Nature, Universe, and suchlike, the

How many brave men have lived before Agamemnon. An
allusion to Horace, *Odes*, IV, ix.
    Igdrasil. The great ash-tree, in Scandinavian mythology,
that stretches its branches over the world; by the spring at its
foot sit the Norns or Fates.

essence of which remains for ever UNNAMEABLE; he who first, gazing into this, fell on his knees awestruck, in silence as is likeliest—he, driven by inner necessity, the 'audacious original' that he was, had done a thing, too, which all thoughtful hearts saw straightway to be an expressive, altogether adoptable thing! To bow the knee was ever since the attitude of supplication. Earlier than any spoken Prayers, *Litanias*, or *Leitourgias*; the beginning of all Worship—which needed by a beginning, so rational was it. What a poet he! Yes, this bold original was a successful one withal. The wellhead this one, hidden in the primeval dusks and distances, from whom as from a Nile-source all *Forms of Worship* flow.

It is all work and forgotten work, this peopled, clothed, articulate-speaking, high-towered, wide-acred World. The hands of forgotten brave men have made it a World for us; they—honour to them; they, in *spite* of the idle and the dastard. This English Land, here and now, is the summary of what was found of wise, and noble, and accordant with God's Truth, in all the generations of English Men. Our English Speech is speakable because there were Hero-Poets of our blood and lineage; speakable in proportion to the number of these. This Land of England has its conquerors, possessors, which change from epoch to epoch, from day to day; but its real conquerors, creators, and eternal proprietors are these following, and their representatives if you can find them: All the Heroic Souls that ever were in England, each in their degree; all the men that

Litanias, or Leitourgias. Litanies and liturgies, set forms of prayer.

ever cut a thistle, drained a puddle out of England,
contrived a wise scheme in England, did or said a true
and valiant thing in England. I tell thee, they had not
a hammer to begin with; and yet Wren built St. Paul's:
not an articulated syllable; and yet there have come
English Literatures, Elizabethan Literatures, Satanic-
School, Cockney-School, and other Literatures—once
more, as in the old time of the *Leitourgia*, a most waste
imbroglio, and world-wide jungle and jumble; waiting
terribly to be 'well-edited' and 'well burnt'! Arachne
started with forefinger and thumb, and had not even a
distaff; yet thou seest Manchester, and Cotton Cloth,
which will shelter naked backs, at twopence an ell.

Work? The quantity of done and forgotten work
that lies silent under my feet in this world, and escorts
and attends me, and supports and keeps me alive,
wheresoever I walk or stand, whatsoever I think or
do, gives rise to reflections! Is it not enough, at any
rate, to strike the thing called 'Fame' into total silence
for a wise man? For fools and unreflective persons,
she is and will be very noisy, this 'Fame', and talks of
her 'immortals' and so forth: but if you will consider it,
what is she? Abbot Samson was not nothing because
nobody *said* anything of him. Or thinkest thou, the
Right Honourable Sir Jabez Windbag can be made

Satanic-School. The name applied by Robert Southey,
Poet Laureate, to Byron and his followers.
Cockney-School. Applied by the reviewers in *Blackwood's
Magazine* to Keats, Leigh Hunt, and others.
Arachne. A Lydian maiden, whose skill in weaving rivalled
that of Athena (Minerva), who out of jealous anger changed her
into a spider.

something by Parliamentary Majorities and Leading
Articles? Her 'immortals'! Scarcely two hundred
years back can Fame recollect articulately at all; and
there she but maunders and mumbles. She manages
to recollect a Shakespeare or so; and prates, considerably
like a goose, about him—and in the rear of that, onwards
to the birth of Theuth, to Hengst's Invasion, and the
bosom of Eternity, it was all blank; and the respectable
Teutonic Languages, Teutonic Practices, Existences, all
came of their own accord, as the grass springs, as the
trees grow; no Poet, no work from the inspired heart of
a Man needed there; and Fame has not an articulate
word to say about it! Or ask her, What, with all
conceivable appliances and mnemonics, including apo-
theosis and human sacrifices among the number, she
carries in her head with regard to a Wodan, even a
Moses, or other such? She begins to be uncertain as
to what they were, whether spirits or men of mould—
gods, charlatans; begins sometimes to have a misgiving
that they were mere symbols, ideas of the mind; perhaps
nonentities and Letters of the Alphabet! She is the
noisiest, inarticulately babbling, hissing, screaming,
foolishest, unmusicalest of fowls that fly; and needs no
'trumpet', I think, but her own enormous goose-throat
—measuring several degrees of celestial latitude, so to
speak. Her 'wings', in these days, have grown far
swifter than ever; but her goose-throat hitherto seems
only larger, louder, and foolisher than ever. *She* is

Theuth. Thoth, an Egyptian god, to whom was attributed
the invention of letters and other arts.
Wodan. Woden or Odin.

transitory, futile, a goose-goddess—if she were not
transitory, what would become of us! It is a chief
comfort that she forgets us all; all, even to the very
Wodans; and grows to consider us, at last, as probably
nonentities and Letters of the Alphabet.

Yes, a noble Abbot Samson resigns himself to Oblivion
too; feels *it* no hardship, but a comfort; counts it as a
still resting-place, from much sick fret and fever and
stupidity, which in the night-watches often made his
strong heart sigh. Your most sweet voices, making
one enormous goose-voice, O Bobus and Company, how
can they be a guidance for any Son of Adam? In
silence of you and the like of you, the 'small still voices'
will speak to him better; in which does lie guidance.

My friend, all speech and rumour is short-lived,
foolish, untrue. Genuine WORK alone, what thou
workest faithfully, that is eternal, as the Almighty
Founder and World-Builder himself. Stand thou by
that; and let 'Fame' and the rest of it go prating.

> Heard are the Voices,
> Heard are the Sages,
> The Worlds and the Ages:
> 'Choose well; your choice is
> Brief and yet endless.
>
> 'Here eyes do regard you,
> In Eternity's stillness;
> Here is all fulness,
> Ye brave, to reward you;
> Work, and despair not.'—GOETHE.

Bobus. Bobus Higgins, 'Sausage-maker on the great scale',
is a character introduced by Carlyle in other parts of *Past
and Present*.

GREAT CHARACTERS

GREAT CHARACTERS

ON HEROES

UNIVERSAL History, the history of what man has accomplished in this world, is at bottom the History of the Great Men who have worked here. They were the leaders of men, these great ones; the modellers, patterns, and in a wide sense creators, of whatsoever the general mass of men contrived to do or to attain; all things that we see standing accomplished in the world are properly the outer material result, the practical realization and embodiment, of Thoughts that dwelt in the Great Men sent into the world: the soul of the whole world's history, it may justly be considered, were the history of these. Too clearly it is a topic we shall do no justice to in this place!

One comfort is, that Great Men, taken up in any way, are profitable company. We cannot look, however imperfectly, upon a great man, without gaining something by him. He is the living light-fountain, which it is good and pleasant to be near. The light which enlightens, which has enlightened the darkness of the world; and this not as a kindled lamp only, but rather as a natural luminary shining by the gift of Heaven; a flowing light-fountain, as I say, of native original insight, of manhood and heroic nobleness;—in whose radiance all souls feel that it is well with them. On any

E   129

terms whatsoever, you will not grudge to wander in such neighbourhood for a while. These Six classes of Heroes, chosen out of widely-distant countries and epochs, and in mere external figure differing altogether, ought, if we look faithfully at them, to illustrate several things for us. Could we see *them* well, we should get some glimpses into the very marrow of the world's history. How happy, could I but, in any measure, in such times as these, make manifest to you the meanings of Heroism; the divine relation (for I may well call it such) which in all times unites a Great Man to other men; and thus, as it were, not exhaust my subject, but so much as break ground on it! At all events, I must make the attempt.

Hero-gods, Prophets, Poets, Priests are forms of Heroism that belong to the old ages, make their appearance in the remotest times; some of them have ceased to be possible long since, and cannot any more show themselves in this world. The Hero as *Man of Letters*, again, is altogether a product of these new ages; and so long as the wondrous art of *Writing*, or of Ready-writing which we call *Printing*, subsists, he may be expected to continue, as one of the main forms of Heroism for all future ages. He is, in various respects, a very singular phenomenon.

There are genuine Men of Letters, and not genuine; as in every kind there is a genuine and a spurious. If

Six classes. The Hero as Divinity, as Prophet, as Poet, as Priest, as Man of Letters, as King; the subjects of six lectures by Carlyle.

Hero be taken to mean genuine, then I say the Hero as Man of Letters will be found discharging a function for us which is ever honourable, ever the highest; and was once well known to be the highest. He is uttering-forth, in such a way as he has, the inspired soul of him; all that a man, in any case, can do. I say *inspired*; for what we call 'originality', 'sincerity', 'genius', the heroic quality we have no good name for, signifies that. The Hero is he who lives in the inward sphere of things, in the True, Divine, and Eternal, which exists always, unseen to most, under the Temporary, Trivial: his being is in that; he declares that abroad, by act or speech as it may be, in declaring himself abroad. His life, as we said before, is a piece of the everlasting heart of Nature herself: all men's life is—but the weak many know not the fact, and are untrue to it, in most times; the strong few are strong, heroic, perennial, because it cannot be hidden from them. The Man of Letters, like every Hero, is there to proclaim this in such sort as he can. Intrinsically it is the same function which the old generations named a man Prophet, Priest, Divinity for doing; which all manner of Heroes, by speech or by act, are sent into the world to do.

SHAKESPEARE

As Dante, the Italian man, was sent into our world
to embody musically the Religion of the Middle Ages,
the Religion of our Modern Europe, its Inner Life; so
Shakespeare, we may say, embodies for us the Outer
Life of our Europe as developed then, its chivalries,
courtesies, humours, ambitions, what practical way of
thinking, acting, looking at the world, men than had.
As in Homer we may still construe Old Greece; so in
Shakespeare and Dante, after thousands of years, what
our modern Europe was, in Faith and in Practice, will
still be legible. Dante has given us the Faith or soul;
Shakespeare, in a not less noble way, has given us the
Practice or body. This latter also we were to have:
a man was sent for it, the man Shakespeare.   Just when
that chivalry way of life had reached its last finish, and
was on the point of breaking down into slow or swift
dissolution, as we now see it everywhere, this other
sovereign Poet, with his seeing eye, with his perennial
singing voice, was sent to take note of it, to give long-
enduring record of it. Two fit men: Dante, deep,
fierce as the central fire of the world; Shakespeare, wide,
placid, far-seeing, as the Sun, the upper light of the
world. Italy produced the one world-voice; we English
had the honour of producing the other.

Dante. The great Italian poet (1265–1321), author of *La
Divina Commedia.*

Curious enough how, as it were by mere accident, this man came to us. I think always, so great, quiet, complete and self-sufficing is this Shakespeare, had the Warwickshire Squire not prosecuted him for deer-stealing, we had perhaps never heard of him as a Poet! The woods and skies, the rustic Life of Man in Stratford there, had been enough for this man! But indeed that strange outbudding of our whole English Existence, which we call the Elizabethan Era, did not it too come as of its own accord? The 'Tree Igdrasil' buds and withers by its own laws—too deep for our scanning. Yet it does bud and wither, and every bough and leaf of it is there, by fixed eternal laws; not a Sir Thomas Lucy but comes at the hour fit for him. Curious, I say, and not sufficiently considered: how everything does co-operate with all; not a leaf rotting on the highway but is indissoluble portion of solar and stellar systems; no thought, word, or act of man but has sprung withal out of all men, and works sooner or later, recognizably or irrecognizably, on all men! It is all a Tree: circulation of sap and influences, mutual communication of every minutest leaf with the lowest talon of a root, with every other greatest and minutest portion of the whole. The Tree Igdrasil, that has its roots down in the Kingdoms of Hela and Death, and whose boughs overspread the highest Heaven!

In some sense it may be said that this glorious

Tree Igdrasil. See note, p. 121.
Sir Thomas Lucy. The story that this Warwickshire squire punished Shakespeare when a youth for poaching was told by Nicholas Rowe, the poet's first biographer, in 1709.

Elizabethan Era with its Shakespeare, as the outcome and flowerage of all which had preceded it, is itself attributable to the Catholicism of the Middle Ages. The Christian Faith, which was the theme of Dante's Song, had produced this Practical Life which Shakespeare was to sing. For Religion then, as it now and always is, was the soul of Practice; the primary vital fact in men's life. And remark here, as rather curious, that Middle-Age Catholicism was abolished, so far as Acts of Parliament could abolish it, before Shakespeare, the noblest product of it, made his appearance. He did make his appearance nevertheless. Nature at her own time, with Catholicism or what else might be necessary, sent him forth; taking small thought of Acts of Parliament. King-Henrys, Queen-Elizabeths go their way; and Nature too goes hers. Acts of Parliament, on the whole, are small, notwithstanding the noise they make. What Act of Parliament, debate at St. Stephen's, on the hustings or elsewhere, was it that brought this Shakespeare into being? No dining at Freemasons' Tavern, opening subscription-lists, selling of shares, and infinite other jangling and true or false endeavouring! This Elizabethan Era, and all its nobleness and blessedness, came without proclamation, preparation of ours. Priceless Shakespeare was the free gift of Nature; given altogether silently—received altogether silently, as if it had been a thing of little account. And yet,

Freemasons' Tavern. In June 1840 Carlyle attended an important meeting here in connection with the founding of the London Library; his speech in support was enthusiastically received.

very literally, it is a priceless thing. One should look at that side of matters too.

Of this Shakespeare of ours, perhaps the opinion one sometimes hears a little idolatrously expressed is, in fact, the right one; I think the best judgment not of this country only, but of Europe at large, is slowly pointing to the conclusion, That Shakespeare is the chief of all Poets hitherto; the greatest intellect who, in our recorded world, has left record of himself in the way of Literature. On the whole, I know not such a power of vision, such a faculty of thought, if we take all the characters of it, in any other man. Such a calmness of depth; placid joyous strength; all things imaged in that great soul of his so true and clear, as in a tranquil unfathomable sea! It has been said, that in the constructing of Shakespeare's Dramas there is, apart from all other 'faculties' as they are called, an understanding manifested, equal to that in Bacon's *Novum Organum*. That is true; and it is not a truth that strikes every one. It would become more apparent if we tried, any of us for himself, how, out of Shakespeare's dramatic materials, *we* could fashion such a result! The built house seems all so fit—everyway as it should be, as if it came there by its own law and the nature of things—we forget the rude disorderly quarry it was shaped from. The very perfection of the house, as if Nature herself had made it, hides the builder's merit. Perfect, more perfect than any other man, we may call Shakespeare in this: he discerns,

Novum Organum. Francis Bacon's great work (in Latin), laying down the principles of scientific method.

knows as by instinct, what conditions he works under, what his materials are, what his own force and its relation to them is. It is not a transitory glance of insight that will suffice; it is deliberate illumination of the whole matter; it is a calmly *seeing* eye; a great intellect, in short. How a man, of some wide thing that he has witnessed, will construct a narrative, what kind of picture and delineation he will give of it—is the best measure you could get of what intellect is in the man. Which circumstance is vital and shall stand prominent; which unessential, fit to be suppressed; where is the true *beginning*, the true sequence and ending? To find out this, you task the whole force of insight that is in the man. He must *understand* the thing; according to the depth of his understanding, will the fitness of his answer be. You will try him so. Does like join itself to like; does the spirit of method stir in that confusion, so that its embroilment becomes order? Can the man say, *Fiat lux*, Let there be light; and out of chaos make a world? Precisely as there is *light* in himself, will he accomplish this.

Or indeed we may say again, it is in what I called Portrait-painting, delineating of men and things, especially of men, that Shakespeare is great. All the greatness of the man comes out decisively here. It is unexampled, I think, that calm creative perspicacity of Shakespeare. The thing he looks at reveals not this or that face of it, but its inmost heart, and generic secret: it dissolves itself as in light before him, so that he discerns the perfect structure of it. Creative, we said: poetic creation, what is this too but *seeing* the thing sufficiently? The *word* that will describe the thing, follows of itself from such clear intense sight of the thing. And is not Shakespeare's *morality*, his valour, candour, tolerance, truthfulness; his whole victorious strength and greatness, which can triumph over such obstructions, visible there too? Great as the world! No *twisted*, poor convex-concave mirror, reflecting all objects with its own convexities and concavities; a perfectly level mirror—that is to say withal, if we will understand it, a man justly related to all things and men, a good man. It is truly a lordly spectacle how this great soul takes-in all kinds of men and objects, a Falstaff, an Othello, a Juliet, a Coriolanus; sets them all forth to us in their round completeness; loving, just, the equal brother of all. *Novum Organum*, and all the intellect you will find in Bacon, is of a quite secondary order; earthy, material, poor in comparison with this. Among modern men, one finds, in strictness, almost nothing of the same rank. Goethe alone, since the days of Shakespeare, reminds me of it. Of him too you say that he *saw* the object; you may say what he himself says of Shakespeare: 'His characters are like watches with dial-plates of transparent crystal; they show you the hour like others, and the inward mechanism also is all visible.'

The seeing eye! It is this that discloses the inner harmony of things; what Nature meant, what musical idea Nature has wrapped-up in these often rough embodiments. Something she did mean. To the

Goethe. German poet-philosopher, died 1832. The quotation is from *Wilhelm Meister*, Book III, chap. xi.

*E

seeing eye that something were discernible. Are they
base, miserable things? You can laugh over them, you
can weep over them; you can in some way or other
genially relate yourself to them—you can, at lowest,
hold your peace about them, turn away your own and
others' face from them, till the hour come for practically
exterminating and extinguishing them! At bottom, it
is the Poet's first gift, as it is all men's, that he have
intellect enough. He will be a Poet if he have: a Poet
in word; or failing that, perhaps still better, a Poet in
act. Whether he write at all; and if so, whether in
prose or in verse, will depend on accidents: who knows
on what extremely trivial accidents—perhaps on his
having had a singing-master, on his being taught to
sing in his boyhood! But the faculty which enables him
to discern the inner heart of things, and the harmony
that dwells there (for whatsoever exists has a harmony
in the heart of it, or it would not hold together and
exist), is not the result of habits or accidents, but the
gift of Nature herself; the primary outfit for a Heroic
Man in what sort soever. To the Poet, as to every
other, we say first of all, *See.* If you cannot do that, it
is of no use to keep stringing rhymes together, jingling
sensibilities against each other, and *name* yourself a
Poet; there is no hope for you. If you can, there is, in
prose or verse, in action or speculation, all manner
of hope.

For, in fact, I say the degree of vision that dwells
in a man is a correct measure of the man. If called
to define Shakespeare's faculty, I should say superiority
of Intellect, and think I had included all under that.

What indeed are faculties? We talk of faculties as if they were distinct, things separable; as if a man had intellect, imagination, fancy, etc., as he has hands, feet, and arms. That is a capital error. Then again, we hear of a man's 'intellectual nature', and of his 'moral nature', as if these again were divisible, and existed apart. Necessities of language do perhaps prescribe such forms of utterance; we must speak, I am aware, in that way, if we are to speak at all. But words ought not to harden into things for us. It seems to me, our apprehension of this matter is, for the most part, radically falsified thereby. We ought to know withal, and to keep for ever in mind, that these divisions are at bottom but *names*; that man's spiritual nature, the vital Force which dwells in him, is essentially one and indivisible; that what we call imagination, fancy, understanding, and so forth, are but different figures of the same Power of Insight, all indissolubly connected with each other, physiognomically related; that if we knew one of them, we might know all of them. Morality itself, what we call the moral quality of a man, what is this but another *side* of the one vital Force whereby he is and works? All that a man does is physiognomical of him. You may see how a man would fight, by the way in which he sings; his courage, or want of courage, is visible in the word he utters, in the opinion he has formed, no less than in the stroke he strikes. He is *one*; and preaches the same Self abroad in all these ways.

If I say, therefore, that Shakespeare is the greatest of Intellects, I have said all concerning him. But there is more in Shakespeare's intellect than we have yet seen. It is what I call an unconscious intellect; there is more virtue in it than he himself is aware of. Novalis beautifully remarks of him, that those Dramas of his are Products of Nature too, deep as Nature herself. I find a great truth in this saying. Shakespeare's Art is not Artifice; the noblest worth of it is not there by plan or precontrivance. It grows-up from the deeps of Nature, through this noble sincere soul, who is a voice of Nature. The latest generations of men will find new meanings in Shakespeare, new elucidations of their own human being; 'new harmonies with the infinite structure of the Universe; concurrences with later ideas, affinities with the higher powers and senses of man'. This well deserves meditating. It is Nature's highest reward to a true simple great soul, that he get thus to be *a part of herself*. Such a man's works, whatsoever he with utmost conscious exertion and forethought shall accomplish, grow up withal *un*consciously, from the unknown deeps in him——as the oak-tree grows from the Earth's bosom, as the mountains and waters shape themselves; with a symmetry grounded on Nature's own laws, conformable to all Truth whatsoever. How much in Shakespeare lies hid; his sorrows, his silent struggles known to himself; much that was not known at all, not speakable at all; like *roots*, like sap and forces working underground! Speech is great; but Silence is greater.

Withal the joyful tranquillity of this man is notable.

Novalis. See note, p. 119.
New harmonies. . . . From Novalis, *Fragments*, 1799.

I will not blame Dante for his misery: it is as battle without victory; but true battle—the first, indispensable thing. Yet I call Shakespeare greater than Dante, in that he fought truly, and did conquer. Doubt it not, he had his own sorrows: those *Sonnets* of his will even testify expressly in what deep waters he had waded, and swum struggling for his life—as what man like him ever failed to have to do? It seems to me a heedless notion, our common one, that he sat like a bird on the bough; and sang forth, free and offhand, never knowing the troubles of other men. Not so; with no man is it so. How could a man travel forward from rustic deer-poaching to such tragedy-writing, and not fall-in with sorrows by the way? Or, still better, how could a man delineate a Hamlet, a Coriolanus, a Macbeth, so many suffering heroic hearts, if his own heroic heart had never suffered? And now, in contrast with all this, observe his mirthfulness, his genuine overflowing love of laughter! You would say, in no point does he *exaggerate* but only in laughter. Fiery objurgations, words that pierce and burn, are to be found in Shakespeare; yet he is always in measure here; never what Johnson would remark as a specially 'good hater'. But his laughter seems to pour from him in floods; he heaps all manner of ridiculous nicknames on the butt he is bantering, tumbles and tosses him in all sorts of horse-play; you would say, with his whole heart laughs.

Sonnets. It is generally held that Shakespeare reveals himself more intimately in his sonnets than elsewhere. Cf. Wordsworth's sonnet, *Scorn not the Sonnet*: 'with this key Shakespeare unlocked his heart'.

And then, if not always the finest, it is always a genial laughter. Not at mere weakness, at misery or poverty; never. No man who *can* laugh, what we call laughing, will laugh at these things. It is some poor character only *desiring* to laugh, and have the credit of wit, that does so. Laughter means sympathy; good laughter is not 'the crackling of thorns under the pot'. Even at stupidity and pretension this Shakespeare does not laugh otherwise than genially. Dogberry and Verges tickle our very hearts; and we dismiss them covered with explosions of laughter: but we like the poor fellows only the better for our laughing; and hope they will get on well there, and continue Presidents of the City-watch. Such laughter, like sunshine on the deep sea, is very beautiful to me.

We have no room to speak of Shakespeare's individual works; though perhaps there is much still waiting to be said on that head. Had we, for instance, all his plays reviewed as *Hamlet*, in *Wilhelm Meister*, is! A thing which might, one day, be done. August Wilhelm Schlegel has a remark on his Historical Plays, *Henry Fifth* and the others, which is worth remembering. He calls them a kind of National Epic. Marlborough, you recollect, said, he knew no English History but what he had learned from Shakespeare. There are really, if we look to it, few as memorable Histories. The great salient points are admirably seized; all rounds itself off,

The crackling of thorns . . . Said of the laughter of a fool (Ecclesiastes vii 6).

Schlegel. A leader of the romantic school in German literature, and translator, with Tieck, of Shakespeare.

into a kind of rhythmic coherence; it is, as Schlegel says, *epic*—as indeed all delineation by a great thinker will be. There are right beautiful things in those Pieces, which indeed together form one beautiful thing. That battle of Agincourt strikes me as one of the most perfect things, in its sort, we anywhere have of Shakespeare's. The description of the two hosts: the worn-out, jaded English; the dread hour, big with destiny, when the battle shall begin; and then that deathless valour: 'Ye good yeomen, whose limbs were made in England!' There is a noble Patriotism in it—far other than the 'indifference' you sometimes hear ascribed to Shakespeare. A true English heart breathes, calm and strong, through the whole business; not boisterous, protrusive; all the better for that. There is a sound in it like the ring of steel. This man too had a right stroke in him, had it come to that!

But I will say, of Shakespeare's works generally, that we have no full impress of him there; even as full as we have of many men. His works are so many windows, through which we see a glimpse of the world that was in him. All his works seem, comparatively speaking, cursory, imperfect, written under cramping circumstances; giving only here and there a note of the full utterance of the man. Passages there are that come upon you like splendour out of Heaven; bursts of radiance, illuminating the very heart of the thing: you say: 'That is *true*, spoken once and forever; wheresoever and whensoever there is an open human soul, that will be recognized as true!' Such bursts, however, make us feel that the surrounding matter is not

radiant; that it is, in part, temporary, conventional.
Alas, Shakespeare had to write for the Globe Play-house:
his great soul had to crush itself, as it could, into that
and no other mould. It was with him, then, as it is
with us all. No man works save under conditions. The
sculptor cannot set his own free Thought before us; but
his Thought as he could translate it into the stone that
was given, with the tools that were given. *Disjecta
membra* are all that we find of any Poet, or of any man.

Whoever looks intelligently at this Shakespeare may
recognize that he too was a *Prophet*, in his way; of an
insight analogous to the Prophetic, though he took it
up in another strain. Nature seemed to this man also
divine; *un*speakable, deep as Tophet, high as Heaven:
'We are such stuff as Dreams are made of!' That
scroll in Westminster Abbey, which few read with
understanding, is of the depth of any seer. But the
man sang; did not preach, except musically. We
called Dante the melodious Priest of Middle - Age
Catholicism. May we not call Shakespeare the still
more melodious Priest of a *true* Catholicism, the
'Universal Church' of the Future and of all times?
No narrow superstition, harsh asceticism, intolerance,
fanatical fierceness or perversion: a Revelation, so far
as it goes, that such a thousandfold hidden beauty and
divineness dwells in all Nature; which let all men worship

Disjecta membra. Scattered fragments.
Scroll in Westminster Abbey. The figure of Shakespeare in
the Poets' Corner carries a scroll inscribed with a passage from
The Tempest, Act IV, sc. i (see p. 43).

as they can! We may say without offence, that there
rises a kind of universal Psalm out of this Shakespeare
too; not unfit to make itself heard among the still more
sacred Psalms. Not in disharmony with these, if we
understood them, but in harmony! I cannot call this
Shakespeare a 'Sceptic', as some do; his indifference to
the creeds and theological quarrels of his time mislead-
ing them. No: neither unpatriotic, though he says
little about his Patriotism; nor sceptic, though he says
little about his Faith. Such 'indifference' was the fruit
of his greatness withal: his whole heart was in his own
grand sphere of worship (we may call it such): these
other controversies, vitally important to other men,
were not vital to him.

But call it worship, call it what you will, is it not
a right glorious thing, and set of things, this that
Shakespeare has brought us? For myself, I feel that
there is actually a kind of sacredness in the fact of such
a man being sent into this Earth. Is he not an eye to
us all; a blessed heaven-sent Bringer of Light? And,
at bottom, was it not perhaps far better that this
Shakespeare, everyway an unconscious man, was *conscious* of no Heavenly message? He did not feel, like
Mahomet, because he saw into those internal Splendours,
that he specially was the 'Prophet of God': and was he
not greater than Mahomet in that? Greater; and also,
if we compute strictly, as we did in Dante's case, more
successful. It was intrinsically an error that notion of
Mahomet's, of his supreme Prophethood: and has come
down to us inextricably involved in error to this day;
dragging along with it such a coil of fables, impurities,

intolerances, as makes it a questionable step for me here and now to say, as I have done, that Mahomet was a true Speaker at all, and not rather an ambitious charlatan, perversity and simulacrum; no Speaker, but a Babbler! Even in Arabia, as I compute, Mahomet will have exhausted himself and become obsolete, while this Shakespeare, this Dante may still be young—while this Shakespeare may still pretend to be a Priest of Mankind, of Arabia as of other places, for unlimited periods to come!

Compared with any speaker or singer one knows, even with Æschylus or Homer, why should he not, for veracity and universality, last like them? He is *sincere* as they; reaches deep down like them, to the universal and perennial. But as for Mahomet, I think it had been better for him *not* to be so conscious! Alas, poor Mahomet; all that he was *conscious* of was a mere error; a futility and triviality—as indeed such ever is. The truly great in him too was the unconscious: that he was a wild Arab lion of the desert, and did speak-out with that great thunder-voice of his, not by words which he *thought* to be great, but by actions, by feelings, by a history which *were* great! His Koran has become a stupid piece of prolix absurdity; we do not believe, like him, that God wrote that! The Great Man here too, as always, is a Force of Nature: whatsoever is truly great in him springs-up from the *in*articulate deeps.

Well: this is our poor Warwickshire Peasant, who

Æschylus. The father of Greek (and hence of European) tragedy, fifth century B.C.

rose to be Manager of a Playhouse, so that he could live without begging; whom the Earl of Southampton cast some kind glances on; whom Sir Thomas Lucy, many thanks to him, was for sending to the Treadmill! We did not account him a god, like Odin, while he dwelt with us—on which point there were much to be said. But I will say rather, or repeat: In spite of the sad state Hero-worship now lies in, consider what this Shakespeare has actually become among us. Which Englishman we ever made, in this land of ours, which million of Englishmen, would we not give-up rather than the Stratford Peasant? There is no regiment of highest Dignitaries that we would sell him for. He is the grandest thing we have yet done. For our honour among foreign nations, as an ornament to our English Household, what item is there that we would not surrender rather than him? Consider now, if they asked us, Will you give-up your Indian Empire or your Shakespeare, you English; never have had any Indian Empire, or never have had any Shakespeare? Really it were a grave question. Official persons would answer doubtless in official language; but we, for our part too, should not we be forced to answer: Indian Empire, or no Indian Empire; we cannot do without Shakespeare! Indian Empire will go, at any rate, some day; but this Shakespeare does not go, he lasts forever with us; we cannot give-up our Shakespeare!

Nay, apart from spiritualities; and considering him merely as a real, marketable, tangibly-useful possession.

Earl of Southampton. Shakespeare's early patron, to whom were dedicated *Venus and Adonis* and *The Rape of Lucrece.*

England, before long, this Island of ours, will hold but
a small fraction of the English: in America, in New
Holland, east and west to the very Antipodes, there will
be a Saxondom covering great spaces of the Globe.
And now, what is it that can keep all these together into
virtually one Nation, so that they do not fall-out and
fight, but live at peace, in brotherlike intercourse,
helping one another? This is justly regarded as the
greatest practical problem, the thing all manner of
sovereignties and governments are here to accomplish:
what is it that will accomplish this? Acts of Parliament, administrative prime ministers cannot. America
is parted from us, so far as Parliament could part it.
Call it not fantastic, for there is much reality in it:
Here, I say, is an English King, whom no time or
chance, Parliament or combination of Parliaments, can
dethrone! This King Shakespeare, does not he shine,
in crowned sovereignty, over us all, as the noblest,
gentlest, yet strongest of rallying-signs; *in*destructible;
really more valuable in that point of view than any
other means or appliance whatsoever? We can fancy
him as radiant aloft over all the Nations of Englishmen,
a thousand years hence. From Paramatta, from New
York, wheresoever, under what sort of Parish-Constable
soever, English men and women are, they will say to
one another: 'Yes, this Shakespeare is ours; we produced him, we speak and think by him; we are of one
blood and kind with him.' The most common-sense
politician, too, if he pleases, may think of that.

Yes, truly, it is a great thing for a Nation that it get
an articulate voice; that it produce a man who will

speak-forth melodiously what the heart of it means!
Italy, for example, poor Italy lies dismembered,
scattered asunder, not appearing in any protocol or
treaty as a unity at all; yet the noble Italy is actually
one: Italy produced its Dante; Italy can speak! The
Czar of all the Russias, he is strong, with so many
bayonets, Cossacks, and cannons; and does a great feat
in keeping such a tract of Earth politically together;
but he cannot yet speak. Something great in him, but
it is a dumb greatness. He has had no voice of genius,
to be heard of all men and times. He must learn to
speak. He is a great dumb monster hitherto. His
cannons and Cossacks will all have rusted into non-
entity, while that Dante's voice is still audible. The
Nation that has a Dante is bound together as no dumb
Russia can be. We must here end what we had to
say of the *Hero-Poet*.

A dumb greatness. At the time when Carlyle was speaking,
Russia had produced no great literature; Tolstoy's first important
work appeared about 1854.

BURNS

IT was a curious phenomenon, in the withered, unbelieving, second-hand Eighteenth Century, that of a Hero
starting up, among the artificial pasteboard figures and
productions, in the guise of a Robert Burns. Like a
little well in the rocky desert places—like a sudden
splendour of Heaven in the artificial Vauxhall! People
knew not what to make of it. They took it for a piece
of the Vauxhall fire-work; alas, it *let* itself be so taken,
though struggling half-blindly, as in bitterness of death,
against that! Perhaps no man had such a false recep-
tion from his fellow-men. Once more a very wasteful
life-drama was enacted under the sun.

The tragedy of Burns's life is known to all of you.
Surely we may say, if discrepancy between place held
and place merited constitute perverseness of lot for a
man, no lot could be more perverse than Burns's.
Among those secondhand acting-figures, *mimes* for most
part, of the Eighteenth Century, once more a giant
Original man; one of those men who reach down to the
perennial Deeps, who take rank with the Heroic among
men: and he was born in a poor Ayrshire hut. The
largest soul of all the British lands came among us in
the shape of a hard-handed Scottish Peasant.

Vauxhall. The gardens here were a centre of fashionable
society; for a good description see Thackeray's *Vanity Fair*,
chap. v. Carlyle takes Vauxhall as symbolic of the artificial
('secondhand') eighteenth century.

His Father, a poor toiling man, tried various things; did not succeed in any; was involved in continual difficulties. The Steward, Factor as the Scotch call him, used to send letters and threatenings, Burns says, 'which threw us all into tears'. The brave, hard-toiling, hard-suffering Father, his brave heroine of a wife; and those children, of whom Robert was one! In this Earth, so wide otherwise, no shelter for *them*. The letters 'threw us all into tears': figure it. The brave Father, I say always—a *silent* Hero and Poet; without whom the son had never been a speaking one! Burns's School-master came afterwards to London, learnt what good society was; but declares that in no meeting of men did he ever enjoy better discourse than at the hearth of this peasant. And his poor 'seven acres of nursery-ground'—not that, nor the miserable patch of clay-farm, nor anything he tried to get a living by, would prosper with him; he had a sore unequal battle all his days. But he stood to it valiantly; a wise, faithful, unconquerable man—swallowing-down how many sore sufferings daily into silence; fighting like an unseen Hero—nobody publishing newspaper paragraphs about his nobleness; voting pieces of plate to him! However, he was not lost: nothing is lost. Robert is there; the outcome of him—and indeed of many generations of such as him.

This Burns appears under every disadvantage: un-instructed, poor, born only to hard manual toil; and writing, when it came to that, in a rustic special dialect, known only to a small province of the country he lived in. Had he written, even what he did write, in the

general language of England, I doubt not he had
already become universally recognized as being, or
capable to be, one of our greatest men. That he should
have tempted so many to penetrate through the rough
husk of that dialect of his, is proof that there lay something far from common within it. He has gained a
certain recognition, and is continuing to do so over all
quarters of our wide Saxon world: wheresoever a
Saxon dialect is spoken, it begins to be understood, by
personal inspection of this and the other, that one of
the most considerable Saxon men of the Eighteenth
Century was an Ayrshire Peasant named Robert Burns.
Yes, I will say, here too was a piece of the right Saxon
stuff: strong as the Harz-rock, rooted in the depths of
the world—rock, yet with wells of living softness in
it! A wild impetuous whirlwind of passion and faculty
slumbered quiet there; such heavenly *melody* dwelling
in the heart of it. A noble rough genuineness; homely,
rustic, honest; true simplicity of strength: with its
lightning-fire, with its soft dewy pity—like the old
Norse Thor, the Peasant-god!

Burns's Brother Gilbert, a man of much sense and
worth, has told me that Robert, in his young days, in
spite of their hardship, was usually the gayest of
speech; a fellow of infinite frolic, laughter, sense, and
heart; far pleasanter to hear there, stript cutting peats
in the bog, or suchlike, than he ever afterwards knew
him. I can well believe it. This basis of mirth ('*fond
gaillard*', as old Marquis Mirabeau calls it), a primal-
element of sunshine and joyfulness, coupled with his
other deep and earnest qualities, is one of the most

attractive characteristics of Burns. A large fund of Hope dwells in him; spite of his tragical history, he is not a mourning man. He shakes his sorrows gallantly aside; bounds forth victorious over them. It is as the lion shaking 'dew-drops from his mane'; as the swift-bounding horse, that *laughs* at the shaking of the spear. But indeed, Hope, Mirth, of the sort like Burns's, are they not the outcome properly of warm generous affection—such as is the beginning of all to every man?

You would think it strange if I called Burns the most gifted British soul we had in all that century of his: and yet I believe the day is coming when there will be little danger in saying so. His writings, all that he *did* under such obstructions, are only a poor fragment of him. Professor Stewart remarked very justly, what indeed is true of all Poets good for much, that his poetry was not any particular faculty; but the general result of a naturally vigorous original mind expressing itself in that way. Burns's gifts, expressed in conversation, are the theme of all that ever heard him. All kinds of gifts: from the gracefulest utterances of courtesy, to the highest fire of passionate speech; loud floods of mirth, soft wailings of affection, laconic emphasis, clear piercing insight; all was in him. Witty duchesses celebrate him as a man whose speech 'led them off their feet'. This is beautiful: but still more beautiful that which Mr. Lockhart has recorded, which I have more than once alluded to, How the waiters and ostlers at

Mr. Lockhart. J. G. Lockhart, son-in-law of Sir Walter Scott, editor of the *Quarterly Review*, and biographer of Scott, and of Burns.

inns would get out of bed, and come crowding to hear this man speak! Waiters and ostlers—they too were men, and here was a man! I have heard much about his speech; but one of the best things I ever heard of it was, last year, from a venerable gentleman long familiar with him. That it was speech distinguished by always *having something in it*. 'He spoke rather little than much,' this old man told me; 'sat rather silent in those early days, as in the company of persons above him; and always when he did speak, it was to throw new light on the matter.' I know not why any one should ever speak otherwise! But if we look at his general force of soul, his healthy *robustness* everyway, the rugged downrightness, penetration, generous valour, and manfulness that was in him—where shall we readily find a better-gifted man?

Among the great men of the Eighteenth Century, I sometimes feel as if Burns might be found to resemble Mirabeau more than any other. They differ widely in vesture; yet look at them intrinsically. There is the same burly thick-necked strength of body as of soul—built, in both cases, on what the old Marquis calls a *fond gaillard*. By nature, by course of breeding, indeed by nation, Mirabeau has much more of bluster; a noisy, forward, unresting man. But the characteristic of Mirabeau too is veracity and sense, power of true *insight*, superiority of vision. The thing that he says is worth remembering. It is a flash of insight into

Mirabeau. One of the leaders of the French Revolution. The Marquis his father wrote on economics and social subjects.

some object or other: so do both these men speak.
The same raging passions; capable too in both of mani-
festing themselves as the tenderest noble affections.
Wit, wild laughter, energy, directness, sincerity: these
were in both. The types of the two men are not dis-
similar. Burns too could have governed, debated in
National Assemblies; politicized, as few could. Alas,
the courage which had to exhibit itself in capture of
smuggling schooners in the Solway Frith; in keeping
silence over so much, where no good speech, but only
inarticulate rage was possible: this might have bellowed
forth Ushers de Brézé and the like; and made itself
visible to all men, in managing of kingdoms, in ruling
of great ever-memorable epochs! But they said to
him reprovingly, his Official Superiors said, and wrote:
'You are to work, not think.' Of your *thinking-*
faculty, the greatest in this land, we have no need; you
are to gauge beer there; for that only are *you* wanted.
Very notable—and worth mentioning, though we know
what is to be said and answered! As if Thought,
Power of Thinking, were not, at all times, in all places
and situations of the world, precisely the thing that
was wanted. The fatal man, is he not always the
*un*thinking man, the man who cannot think and *see*;
but only grope, and hallucinate, and *mis*see the nature
of the thing he works with? He missees it, mis*takes*
it as we say; takes it for one thing, and it *is* another
thing—and leaves him standing like a Futility there!
He is the fatal man; unutterably fatal, put in the high

Smuggling schooners. Burns was appointed an exciseman in
1788.

places of men. 'Why complain of this?' say some:
'Strength is mournfully denied its arena; that was true
from of old.' Doubtless; and the worse for the *arena*,
answer I! *Complaining* profits little; stating of the truth
may profit. That a Europe, with its French Revolution
just breaking out, finds no need of a Burns except for
gauging beer—is a thing I, for one, cannot *rejoice* at!

Once more we have to say here, that the chief quality
of Burns is the *sincerity* of him. So in his Poetry, so
in his Life. The Song he sings is not of fantasticalities;
it is of a thing felt, really there; the prime merit of this,
as of all in him, and of his Life generally, is truth.
The Life of Burns is what we may call a great tragic
sincerity. A sort of savage sincerity—not cruel, far
from that; but wild, wrestling naked with the truth
of things. In that sense, there is something of the
savage in all great men.

Hero-worship—Odin, Burns? Well; these Men of
Letters too were not without a kind of Hero-worship:
but what a strange condition has that got into now!
The waiters and ostlers of Scotch inns, prying about
the door, eager to catch any word that fell from Burns,
were doing unconscious reverence to the Heroic. Johnson had his Boswell for worshipper. Rousseau had
worshippers enough; princes calling on him in his mean
garret; the great, the beautiful doing reverence to the
poor moonstruck man. For himself a most portentous
contradiction; the two ends of his life not to be brought
into harmony. He sits at the tables of grandees; and
has to copy music for his own living. He cannot even
get his music copied. 'By dint of dining out,' says

he, 'I run the risk of dying by starvation at home.'
For his worshippers too a most questionable thing! If
doing Hero-worship well or badly be the test of vital
well-being or ill-being to a generation, can we say that
these generations are very first-rate? And yet our
heroic Men of Letters do teach, govern, are kings,
priests, or what you like to call them; intrinsically
there is no preventing it by any means whatever. The
world *has* to obey him who thinks and sees in the
world. The world can alter the manner of that; can
either have it as blessed continuous summer sunshine,
or as unblessed black thunder and tornado—with unspeakable difference of profit for the world! The
manner of it is very alterable; the matter and fact of
it is not alterable by any power under the sky. Light;
or, failing that, lightning: the world can take its choice.
Not whether we call an Odin god, prophet, priest, or
what we call him; but whether we believe the word he
tells us: there it all lies. If it be a true word, we shall
have to believe it; believing it, we shall have to do it.
What *name* or welcome we give him or it, is a point that
concerns ourselves mainly. *It*, the new Truth, new
deeper revealing of the Secret of this Universe, is verily
of the nature of a message from on high; and must and
will have itself obeyed.

My last remark is on that notablest phasis of Burns's
history—his visit to Edinburgh. Often it seems to me

Visit to Edinburgh. After the successful publication of his
first volume of poems, in 1786, Burns was invited to Edinburgh,
and there *lionized* as Carlyle describes. He had been on the
point of fleeing to Jamaica to escape the consequences of extreme
poverty.

as if his demeanour there were the highest proof he
gave of what a fund of worth and genuine manhood
was in him. If we think of it, few heavier burdens
could be laid on the strength of a man. So sudden;
all common *Lionism*, which ruins innumerable men,
was as nothing to this. It is as if Napoleon had been
made a King of, not gradually, but at once from the
Artillery Lieutenancy in the Regiment La Fère. Burns,
still only in his twenty-seventh year, is no longer even
a ploughman; he is flying to the West Indies to escape
disgrace and a jail. This month he is a ruined peasant,
his wages seven pounds a year, and these gone from
him: next month he is in the blaze of rank and beauty,
handing down jewelled Duchesses to dinner; the
cynosure of all eyes! Adversity is sometimes hard
upon a man; but for one man who can stand prosperity,
there are a hundred that will stand adversity. I admire
much the way in which Burns met all this. Perhaps
no man one could point out, was ever so sorely tried,
and so little forgot himself. Tranquil, unastonished;
not abashed, not inflated, neither awkwardness nor
affectation: he feels that *he* there is the man Robert
Burns; that the 'rank is but the guinea-stamp'; that
the celebrity is but the candle-light, which will show
what man, not in the least make him a better or other
man! Alas, it may readily, unless he look to it, make
him a *worse* man; a wretched inflated wind-bag—
inflated till he *burst*, and become a *dead* lion; for
whom, as some one has said, 'there is no resurrection
of the body'; worse than a living dog! Burns is
admirable here.

And yet, alas, as I have observed elsewhere, these Lion-hunters were the ruin and death of Burns. It was they that rendered it impossible for him to live! They gathered round him in his Farm; hindered his industry; no place was remote enough from them. He could not get his Lionism forgotten, honestly as he was disposed to do so. He falls into discontents, into miseries, faults; the world getting ever more desolate for him; health, character, peace of mind all gone—solitary enough now. It is tragical to think of! These men came but to *see* him; it was out of no sympathy with him, nor no hatred to him. They came to get a little amusement: they got their amusement—and the Hero's life went for it!

Richter says, in the Island of Sumatra, there is a kind of 'Light-chafers', large Fire-flies, which people stick upon spits, and illuminate the ways with at night. Persons of condition can thus travel with a pleasant radiance, which they much admire. Great honour to the Fire-flies! But——!

JOHNSON

As for Johnson, I have always considered him to be,
by nature, one of our great English souls. A strong
and noble man; so much left undeveloped in him to
the last: in a kindlier element what might he not have
been—Poet, Priest, sovereign Ruler! On the whole, a
man must not complain of his 'element', of his 'time',
or the like; it is thriftless work doing so. His time is
bad: well then, he is there to make it better! Johnson's
youth was poor, isolated, hopeless, very miserable.
Indeed, it does not seem possible that, in any the
favourablest outward circumstances, Johnson's life
could have been other than a painful one. The world
might have had more of profitable *work* out of him, or
less; but his *effort* against the world's work could never
have been a light one. Nature, in return for his nobleness, had said to him, Live in an element of diseased
sorrow. Nay, perhaps the sorrow and the nobleness
were intimately and even inseparably connected with
each other. At all events, poor Johnson had to go
about girt with continual hypochondria, physical and
spiritual pain. Like a Hercules with the burning
Nessus'-shirt on him, which shoots-in on him dull

Nessus'-shirt. The shirt, stained with the blood of the
Centaur, Nessus, that was given by Deianira to her husband
Hercules in order to retain his affections; the blood had been
poisoned by the arrow with which Hercules had killed the
Centaur, so that Hercules died in agony.

incurable misery: the Nessus'-shirt not to be stript-off, which is his own natural skin! In this manner *he* had to live. Figure him there, with his scrofulous diseases, with his great greedy heart, and unspeakable chaos of thoughts; stalking mournful as a stranger in this Earth; eagerly devouring what spiritual thing he could come at: school-languages and other merely grammatical stuff, if there were nothing better! The largest soul that was in all England; and provision made for it of 'fourpence-halfpenny a day'. Yet a giant invincible soul; a true man's. One remembers always that story of the shoes at Oxford: the rough, seamy-faced, rawboned College Servitor stalking about, in winter-season, with his shoes worn-out; how the charitable Gentleman Commoner secretly places a new pair at his door; and the raw-boned Servitor, lifting them, looking at them near, with his dim eyes, with what thoughts—pitches them out of window! Wet feet, mud, frost, hunger or what you will; but not beggary: we cannot stand beggary! Rude stubborn self-help here; a whole world of squalor, rudeness, confused misery, and want, yet of nobleness and manfulness withal. It is a type of the man's life, this pitching-away of the shoes. An original man—not a secondhand, borrowing or begging man. Let us stand on our own basis, at any rate! On such shoes as we ourselves can get. On frost and mud, if you will, but honestly on that—on the reality and substance which Nature gives *us*, not on the semblance, on the thing she has given another than us!

And yet with all this rugged pride of manhood and self-help, was there ever soul more tenderly affectionate,

loyally submissive to what was really higher than he?
Great souls are always loyally submissive, reverent to
what is over them; only small mean souls are otherwise.
I could not find a better proof of what I said the other
day, That the sincere man was by nature the obedient
man; that only in a World of Heroes was there loyal
Obedience to the Heroic. The essence of *originality*
is not that it be *new*: Johnson believed altogether in
the old; he found the old opinions credible for him, fit
for him; and in a right heroic manner lived under them.
He is well worth study in regard to that. For we are
to say that Johnson was far other than a mere man of
words and formulas; he was a man of truths and facts.
He stood by the old formulas; the happier was it for
him that he could so stand: but in all formulas that
he could stand by, there needed to be a most genuine
substance. Very curious how, in that poor Paper-age,
so barren, artificial, thick-quilted with Pedantries, Hear-
says, the great Fact of this Universe glared in, forever
wonderful, indubitable, unspeakable, divine-infernal,
upon this man too! How he harmonized his Formulas
with it, how he managed at all under such circumstances:
that is a thing worth seeing. A thing 'to be looked at
with reverence, with pity, with awe'. That Church of
St. Clement Danes, where Johnson still *worshipped* in
the era of Voltaire, is to me a venerable place.

It was in virtue of his *sincerity*, of his speaking still
in some sort from the heart of Nature, though in the
current artificial dialect, that Johnson was a Prophet.

St. Clement Danes. The church in the Strand, where Johnson
regularly worshipped.

Are not all dialects 'artificial'? Artificial things are
not all false—nay every true Product of Nature will
infallibly *shape* itself; we may say all artificial things
are, at the starting of them, *true*. What we call
'Formulas' are not in their origin bad; they are indis-
pensably good. Formula is *method*, habitude; found
wherever man is found. Formulas fashion themselves
as Paths do, as beaten Highways, leading towards some
sacred or high object, whither many men are bent.

Mark, too, how little Johnson boasts of his 'sincerity'.
He has no suspicion of his being particularly sincere—
of his being particularly anything! A hard-struggling,
weary-hearted man, or 'scholar' as he calls himself,
trying hard to get some honest livelihood in the world,
not to starve, but to live—without stealing! A noble
unconsciousness is in him. He does not 'engrave *Truth*
on his watch-seal'; no, but he stands by truth, speaks
by it, works and lives by it. Thus it ever is. Think
of it once more. The man whom Nature has appointed
to do great things is, first of all, furnished with that
openness to Nature which renders him incapable of
being *in*sincere! To this large, open, deep-feeling heart
Nature is a Fact: all hearsay is hearsay; the unspeakable
greatness of this Mystery of Life, let him acknowledge
it or not, nay even though he seem to forget it or deny
it, is ever present to *him*—fearful and wonderful, on
this hand and on that. He has a basis of sincerity;
unrecognized, because never questioned or capable of
question. Mirabeau, Mahomet, Cromwell, Napoleon:
all the Great Men I ever heard-of have this as the
primary material of them. Innumerable commonplace

men are debating, are talking everywhere their commonplace doctrines, which they have learned by logic, by
rote, at secondhand: to that kind of man all this is
still nothing. He must have truth; truth which *he*
feels to be true. How shall he stand otherwise? His
whole soul, at all moments, in all ways, tells him that
there is no standing. He is under the noble necessity
of being true. Johnson's way of thinking about this
world is not mine, any more than Mahomet's was: but
I recognize the everlasting element of heart-*sincerity* in
both; and see with pleasure how neither of them remains
ineffectual. Neither of them is as *chaff* sown; in both
of them is something which the seed-field will *grow*.

Johnson was a Prophet to his people; preached a
Gospel to them—as all like him always do. The highest
Gospel he preached we may describe as a kind of Moral
Prudence: 'in a world where much is to be done, and
little is to be known', see how you will *do* it! A thing
well worth preaching. 'A world where much is to be
done, and little is to be known': do not sink yourselves
in boundless bottomless abysses of Doubt, of wretched
god-forgetting Unbelief — you were miserable then,
powerless, mad: how could you *do* or work at all?
Such Gospel Johnson preached and taught—coupled,
theoretically and practically, with this other great
Gospel, 'Clear your mind of Cant!' Have no trade
with Cant: stand on the cold mud in the frosty weather,
but let it be in your own *real* torn shoes: 'that will be
better for you', as Mahomet says! I call this, I call
these two things *joined together*, a great Gospel, the
greatest perhaps that was possible at that time.

Johnson's Writings, which once had such currency and celebrity, are now, as it were, disowned by the young generation. It is not wonderful; Johnson's opinions are fast becoming obsolete: but his style of thinking and of living, we may hope, will never become obsolete. I find in Johnson's Books the indisputablest traces of a great intellect and great heart—ever welcome, under what obstructions and perversions soever. They are *sincere* words, those of his; he means things by them. A wondrous buckram style—the best he could get to then; a measured grandiloquence, stepping or rather stalking along in a very solemn way, grown obsolete now; sometimes a tumid *size* of phraseology not in proportion to the contents of it: all this you will put-up with. For the phraseology, tumid or not, has always *something within it*. So many beautiful styles and books, with *nothing* in them—a man is a *male*factor to the world who writes such! *They* are the avoidable kind! Had Johnson left nothing but his *Dictionary*, one might have traced there a great intellect, a genuine man. Looking to its clearness of definition, its general solidity, honesty, insight, and successful method, it may be called the best of all Dictionaries. There is in it a kind of architectural nobleness; it stands there like a great solid square-built edifice, finished, symmetrically complete: you judge that a true Builder did it.

One word, in spite of our haste, must be granted to poor Bozzy. He passes for a mean, inflated, gluttonous creature; and was so in many senses. Yet the fact of his reverence for Johnson will ever remain noteworthy. The foolish conceited Scotch Laird, the most conceited

man of his time, approaching in such awestruck attitude
the great dusty irascible Pedagogue in his mean garret
there: it is a genuine reverence for Excellence; a *worship*
for Heroes, at a time when neither Heroes nor worship
were surmised to exist. Heroes, it would seem, exist
always, and a certain worship of them! We will also
take the liberty to deny altogether that of the witty
Frenchman, that no man is a Hero to his valet-de-
chambre. Or if so, it is not the Hero's blame, but the
Valet's: that his soul, namely, is a mean *valet*-soul!
He expects his Hero to advance in royal stage-trappings,
with measured step, trains borne behind him, trumpets
sounding before him. It should stand rather, No man
can be a *Grand-Monarque* to his valet-de-chambre.
Strip your Louis Quatorze of his king-gear, and there
is left nothing but a poor forked radish with a head
fantastically carved—admirable to no valet. The
Valet does not know a Hero when he sees him! Alas,
no: it requires a kind of *Hero* to do that—and one of
the world's wants, in *this* as in other senses, is for the
most part want of such.

On the whole, shall we not say, that Boswell's admiration was well bestowed; that he could have found no
soul in all England so worthy of bending down before?
Shall we not say, of this great mournful Johnson too,
that he guided his difficult confused existence wisely;
led it *well*, like a right-valiant man? That waste chaos

Forked radish. An allusion to *Henry IV*, Part II, Act III
sc. ii: 'Like a man made after supper of a cheese-paring: when
'a was naked he was for all the world like a forked radish, with a
head fantastically carved upon it with a knife'.

of Authorship by trade; that waste chaos of Scepticism in religion and politics, in life-theory and life-practice; in his poverty, in his dust and dimness, with the sick body and the rusty coat: he made it do for him, like a brave man. Not wholly without a loadstar in the Eternal; he had still a loadstar, as the brave all need to have: with his eye set on that, he would change his course for nothing in these confused vortices of the lower sea of Time. 'To the Spirit of Lies, bearing death and hunger, he would in no wise strike his flag.' Brave old Samuel: *ultimus Romanorum!*

COLERIDGE

(From *The Life of John Sterling*)

COLERIDGE sat on the brow of Highgate Hill, in those years, looking down on London and its smoke-tumult, like a sage escaped from the inanity of life's battle; attracting towards him the thoughts of innumerable brave souls still engaged there. His express contributions to poetry, philosophy, or any specific province of human literature or enlightenment, had been small and sadly intermittent; but he had, especially among young inquiring men, a higher than literary, a kind of prophetic or magician character. He was thought to hold, he alone in England, the key of German and other Transcendentalisms; knew the sublime secret of believing by 'the reason' what 'the understanding' had been obliged to fling out as incredible; and could still, after Hume and Voltaire had done their best and worst with him, profess himself an orthodox Christian, and say and print to the Church of England, with its singular old rubrics and surplices at Allhallowtide, *Esto perpetua*. A sublime man; who, alone in those dark days, had

Highgate Hill. The poet resided here with Dr. Gilman from 1816 till his death in 1834.

Transcendentalisms. Idealist philosophies.

Hume and Voltaire. Eighteenth - century philosophers, 'rationalists'.

Esto perpetua. Endure for ever.

saved his crown of spiritual manhood; escaping from
the black materialisms, and revolutionary deluges, with
'God, Freedom, Immortality' still his: a king of men.
The practical intellects of the world did not much heed
him, or carelessly reckoned him a metaphysical dreamer:
but to the rising spirits of the young generation he
had this dusky sublime character; and sat there as
a kind of *Magus*, girt in mystery and enigma; his
Dodona oak-grove (Mr. Gilman's house at Highgate)
whispering strange things, uncertain whether oracles
or jargon.

The Gilmans did not encourage much company, or
excitation of any sort, round their sage; nevertheless
access to him, if a youth did reverently wish it, was
not difficult. He would stroll about the pleasant garden
with you, sit in the pleasant rooms of the place—perhaps take you to his own peculiar room, high up, with
a rearward view, which was the chief view of all.
A really charming outlook, in fine weather. Close at
hand, wide sweep of flowery leafy gardens, their few
houses mostly hidden, the very chimney-pots veiled
under blossomy umbrage, flowed gloriously down hill;
gloriously issuing in wide-tufted undulating plain
country, rich in all charms of field and town. Waving
blooming country of the brightest green; dotted all
over with handsome villas, handsome groves; crossed
by roads and human traffic, here inaudible or heard
only as a musical hum: and behind all swam, under
olive-tinted haze, the illimitable limitary ocean of

Dodona oak-grove. Dodona was the most ancient oracle in
Greece, situated in Epirus.

London, with its domes and steeples definite in the sun, big Paul's and the many memories attached to it hanging high over all. Nowhere, of its kind, could you see a grander prospect on a bright summer day, with the set of the air going southward—southward, and so draping with the city smoke not *you* but the city. Here for hours would Coleridge talk, concerning all conceivable or inconceivable things; and liked nothing better than to have an intelligent, or failing that, even a silent and patient human listener. He distinguished himself to all that ever heard him as at least the most surprising talker extant in this world—and to some small minority, by no means to all, as the most excellent.

The good man, he was now getting old, towards sixty perhaps; and gave you the idea of a life that had been full of sufferings; a life heavy-laden, half-vanquished, still swimming painfully in seas of manifold physical and other bewilderment. Brow and head were round, and of massive weight, but the face was flabby and irresolute. The deep eyes, of a light hazel, were as full of sorrow as of inspiration; confused pain looked mildly from them, as in a kind of mild astonishment. The whole figure and air, good and amiable otherwise, might be called flabby and irresolute; expressive of weakness under possibility of strength. He hung loosely on his limbs, with knees bent, and stooping attitude; in walking, he rather shuffled than decisively stept; and a lady once remarked, he never could fix which side of the garden walk would suit him best, but continually shifted, in corkscrew fashion, and kept trying both. A heavy-laden, high-aspiring and surely much-suffering

man. His voice, naturally soft and good, had con-
tracted itself into a plaintive snuffle and singsong; he
spoke as if preaching—you would have said, preaching
earnestly and also hopelessly the weightiest things.
I still recollect his 'object' and 'subject', terms of
continual recurrence in the Kantean province; and how
he sang and snuffled them into 'om-m-mject' and
'sum-m-mject', with a kind of solemn shake or quaver,
as he rolled along. No talk, in his century or in any
other, could be more surprising.

Furthermore it was always, virtually or literally, of
the nature of a monologue; suffering no interruption,
however reverent; hastily putting aside all foreign addi-
tions, annotations, or most ingenuous desires for elucida-
tion, as well-meant superfluities which would never do.
Besides, it was talk not flowing anywhither like a river,
but spreading everywhither in inextricable currents and
regurgitations like a lake or sea; terribly deficient in
definite goal or aim, nay often in logical intelligibility;
what you were to believe or do, on any earthly
or heavenly thing, obstinately refusing to appear
from it. So that, most times, you felt logically lost;
swamped near to drowning in this tide of ingenious
vocables, spreading out boundless as if to submerge the
world.

To sit as a passive bucket and be pumped into,
whether you consent or not, can in the long run be
exhilarating to no creature; how eloquent soever the
flood of utterance that is descending. But if it be

Kantean province. The philosophy of Immanuel Kant
(1724–1804).

withal a confused unintelligible flood of utterance,
threatening to submerge all known landmarks of thought,
and drown the world and you!—I have heard Coleridge
talk, with eager musical energy, two stricken hours, his
face radiant and moist, and communicate no meaning
whatsoever to any individual of his hearers—certain
of whom, I for one, still kept eagerly listening in hope;
the most had long before given up, and formed (if the
room were large enough) secondary humming groups
of their own. He began anywhere: you put some
question to him, made some suggestive observation:
instead of answering this, or decidedly setting out
towards answer of it, he would accumulate formidable
apparatus, logical swim-bladders, transcendental life-
preservers and other precautionary and vehiculatory
gear, for setting out; perhaps did at last get under way
—but was swiftly solicited, turned aside by the glance
of some radiant new game on this hand or that, into
new courses; and ever into new; and before long into
all the Universe, where it was uncertain what game
you would catch, or whether any.

Glorious islets, too, I have seen rise out of the haze;
but they were few, and soon swallowed in the general
element again. Balmy sunny islets, islets of the blest
and the intelligible—on which occasions those secondary
humming groups would all cease humming, and hang
breathless upon the eloquent words; till once your islet
got wrapt in the mist again, and they could recommence
humming. Eloquent artistically expressive words you
always had; piercing radiances of a most subtle insight
came at intervals; tones of noble pious sympathy,

recognizable as pious though strangely coloured, were never wanting long: but in general you could not call this aimless, cloudcapt, cloudbased, lawlessly meandering human discourse of reason by the name of 'excellent talk', but only of 'surprising'; and were reminded bitterly of Hazlitt's account of it: 'Excellent talker, very—if you let him start from no premises and come to no conclusion'. Coleridge was not without what talkers call wit, and there were touches of prickly sarcasm in him, contemptuous enough of the world and its idols and popular dignitaries; he had traits even of poetic humour: but in general he seemed deficient in laughter; or indeed in sympathy for concrete human things either on the sunny or on the stormy side. One right peal of concrete laughter at some convicted flesh-and-blood absurdity, one burst of noble indignation at some injustice or depravity, rubbing elbows with us on this solid Earth, how strange would it have been in that Kantean haze-world, and how infinitely cheering amid its vacant air-castles and dim-melting ghosts and shadows! None such ever came. His life had been an abstract thinking and dreaming, idealistic, passed amid the ghosts of defunct bodies and of unborn ones. The moaning singsong of that theosophico-metaphysical monotony left on you, at last, a very dreary feeling.

The truth is, I now see, Coleridge's talk and speculation was the emblem of himself: in it as in him, a ray of heavenly inspiration struggled, in a tragically ineffectual degree, with the weakness of flesh and blood. He says once, he 'had skirted the howling deserts of

Infidelity'; this was evident enough: but he had not had the courage, in defiance of pain and terror, to press resolutely across said deserts to the new firm lands of Faith beyond; he preferred to create logical fatamorganas for himself on this hither side, and laboriously solace himself with these.

To the man himself Nature had given, in high measure, the seeds of a noble endowment; and to unfold it had been forbidden him. A subtle lynx-eyed intellect, tremulous pious sensibility to all good and all beautiful; truly a ray of empyrean light—but imbedded in such weak laxity of character, in such indolences and esuriences as had made strange work with it. Once more, the tragic story of a high endowment with an insufficient will. An eye to discern the divineness of the Heaven's splendours and lightnings, the insatiable wish to revel in their godlike radiances and brilliances; but no heart to front the scathing terrors of them, which is the first condition of your conquering an abiding place there. The courage necessary for him, above all things, had been denied this man. His life, with such ray of the empyrean in it, was great and terrible to him; and he had not valiantly grappled with it, he had fled from it; sought refuge in vague day-dreams, hollow compromises, in opium, in theosophic metaphysics. Harsh pain, danger, necessity, slavish harnessed toil, were of all things abhorrent to him. And so the empyrean element, lying smothered under the terrene, and yet inextinguishable there, made sad writhings. For pain, danger, difficulty, steady slaving toil, and other highly disagreeable behests of destiny, shall in no wise be shirked by any brightest mortal that will approve himself loyal to his mission in this world; nay, precisely the higher he is, the deeper will be the disagreeableness, and the detestability to flesh and blood, of the tasks laid on him; and the heavier too, and more tragic, his penalties if he neglect them.

CROMWELL

In the age which directly followed that of the Puritans, their cause or themselves were little likely to have justice done them. Charles Second and his Rochesters were not the kind of men you would set to judge what the worth or meaning of such men might have been. That there could be any faith or truth in the life of a man, was what these poor Rochesters, and the age they ushered-in, had forgotten. Puritanism was hung on gibbets—like the bones of the leading Puritans. Its work nevertheless went on accomplishing itself. All true work of a man, hang the author of it on what gibbet you like, must and will accomplish itself. We have our *Habeas-Corpus*, our free Representation of the People; acknowledgment, wide as the world, that all men are, or else must, shall, and will become, what we call *free* men—men with their life grounded on reality and justice, not on tradition, which has become unjust and a chimera! This in part and much besides this, was the work of the Puritans.

Few Puritans of note but find their apologists somewhere, and have a certain reverence paid them by earnest men. One Puritan, I think, and almost he

Rochesters. John Wilmot, Earl of Rochester, was the notorious patron and leader of the Restoration gallants.
Habeas Corpus. An Act passed in 1679 to secure speedy trial of accused persons.

alone, our poor Cromwell, seems to hang yet on the gibbet, and find no hearty apologist anywhere. Him neither saint nor sinner will acquit of great wickedness. A man of ability, infinite talent, courage, and so forth: but he betrayed the Cause. Selfish ambition, dishonesty, duplicity; a fierce, coarse, hypocritical *Tartufe*; turning all that noble Struggle for constitutional Liberty into a sorry farce played for his own benefit: this and worse is the character they give of Cromwell. And then there come contrasts with Washington and others; above all, with these noble Pyms and Hampdens, whose noble work he stole for himself, and ruined into a futility and deformity.

From of old, I will confess, this theory of Cromwell's falsity has been incredible to me. Nay I cannot believe the like, of any Great Man whatever. Multitudes of Great Men figure in History as false selfish men; but if we will consider it, they are but *figures* for us, unintelligible shadows; we do not see into them as men that could have existed at all. A superficial unbelieving generation only, with no eye but for the surfaces and semblances of things, could form such notions of Great Men. Can a great soul be possible without a *conscience* in it, the essence of all *real* souls, great or small? No, we cannot figure Cromwell as a Falsity and Fatuity; the longer I study him and his career, I believe this the less.

Tartufe. The leading character of Molière's play of that title; a hypocrite.

Pyms and Hampdens. John Pym and John Hampden, representative 'heroes' of the parliamentary party in Charles I's reign.

Looking at the man's life with our own eyes, it seems to me, a very different hypothesis suggests itself. What little we know of his earlier obscure years, distorted as it has come down to us, does it not all betoken an earnest, affectionate, sincere kind of man? His nervous melancholic temperament indicates rather a seriousness *too* deep for him. Of those stories of 'Spectres'; of the white Spectre in broad daylight, predicting that he should be King of England, we are not bound to believe much—probably no more than of the other black Spectre, or Devil in person, to whom the Officer *saw* him sell himself before Worcester Fight! But the mournful, over-sensitive, hypochondriac humour of Oliver, in his young years, is otherwise indisputably known. The Huntingdon Physician told Sir Philip Warwick himself, He had often been sent for at midnight; Mr. Cromwell was full of hypochondria, thought himself near dying, and 'had fancies about the Town-cross'. These things are significant. Such an excitable deep-feeling nature, in that rugged stubborn strength of his, is not the symptom of falsehood; it is the symptom and promise of quite other than falsehood!

The young Oliver is sent to study Law; falls, or is said to have fallen, for a little period, into some of the dissipations of youth; but if so, speedily repents, abandons all this: not much above twenty, he is married, settled as an altogether grave and quiet man. 'He pays-back what money he had won at gambling,' says the story—he does not think any gain of that kind

Worcester Fight. Cromwell's victory in 1651, when the Scottish and English royalists were finally subdued.

could be really *his*. It is very interesting, very natural, this 'conversion', as they well name it; this awakening of a great true soul from the worldly slough, to see into the awful *truth* of things—to see that time and its shows all rested on Eternity, and this poor Earth of ours was the threshold either of Heaven or of Hell! Oliver's life at St. Ives or Ely, as a sober industrious Farmer, is it not altogether as that of a true and devout man? He has renounced the world and its ways; *its* prizes are not the thing that can enrich him. He tills the earth; he reads his Bible; daily assembles his servants round him to worship God. He comforts persecuted ministers, is fond of preachers; nay can himself preach—exhorts his neighbours to be wise, to redeem the time. In all this what 'hypocrisy', 'ambition', 'cant', or other falsity? The man's hopes, I do believe, were fixed on the other Higher World; his aim to get well *thither*, by walking well through his humble course in *this* world. He courts no notice: what could notice here do for him? 'Ever in his great Taskmaster's eye.'

It is striking, too, how he comes-out once into public view; he, since no other is willing to come: in resistance to a public grievance. I mean, in that matter of the Bedford Fens. No one else will go to law with Authority; therefore he will. That matter once settled, he returns back into obscurity, to his Bible and his Plough. 'Gain influence'? His influence is the most legitimate;

'*Ever . . . eye.*' Quoted from Milton's sonnet: *On his having arrived at the age of twenty-three years.*

Bedford Fens. Cromwell in his earlier days had successfully led local opposition to the government in the draining of these fens.

derived from personal knowledge of him, as a just, religious, reasonable, and determined man. In this way he has lived till past forty; old age is now in view of him, and the earnest portal of Death and Eternity; it was at this point that he suddenly became 'ambitious'! I do not interpret his Parliamentary mission in that way!

His successes in Parliament, his successes through the war, are honest successes of a brave man; who has more resolution in the heart of him, more light in the head of him than other men. His prayers to God; his spoken thanks to the God of Victory, who had pre-served him safe, and carried him forward so far, through the furious clash of a world all set in conflict, through desperate-looking envelopments at Dunbar; through the death-hail of so many battles; mercy after mercy; to the 'crowning mercy' of Worcester Fight: all this is good and genuine for a deep-hearted Calvinistic Crom-well. Only to vain unbelieving Cavaliers, worshipping not God but their own 'lovelocks', frivolities, and formalities, living quite apart from contemplations of God, living *without* God in the world, need it seem hypocritical.

Nor will his participation in the King's death involve him in condemnation with us. It is a stern business killing of a King! But if you once go to war with him, it lies *there*; this and all else lies there. Once at war, you have made wager of battle with him: it is he to die, or else you. Reconciliation is problematic; may be possible, or, far more likely, is impossible. It is now pretty generally admitted that the Parliament, having vanquished Charles First, had no way of making any

Dunbar. Victory of Cromwell over the Scots in 1650.

tenable arrangement with him. The large Presbyterian
party, apprehensive now of the Independents, were
most anxious to do so; anxious indeed as for their own
existence; but it could not be. The unhappy Charles,
in those final Hampton Court negotiations, shows himself as a many fatally incapable of being dealt with.
A man who, once for all, could not and would not
understand—whose thought did not in any measure
represent to him the real fact of the matter; nay worse,
whose *word* did not at all represent his thought. We
may say this of him without cruelty, with deep pity
rather: but it is true and undeniable. Forsaken there
of all but the *name* of Kingship, he still, finding himself
treated with outward respect as a King, fancied that he
might play-off party against party, and smuggle himself
into his old power by deceiving both. Alas, they both
discovered that he was deceiving them. A man whose
word will not inform you at all what he means or will
do, is not a man you can bargain with. You must get
out of that man's way, or put him out of yours! The
Presbyterians, in their despair, were still for believing
Charles, though found false, unbelievable again and
again. Not so Cromwell: 'For all our fighting,' says he,
'we are to have a little bit of paper?' No!—

In fact, everywhere we have to note the decisive
practical *eye* of this man; how he drives towards the
practical and practicable; has a genuine insight into
what *is* fact. Such an intellect, I maintain, does not

Hampton Court negotiations. Abortive parleys in 1647. Charles
fled from the conference hoping to escape to France, but was
captured and confined in Carisbrooke Castle, Isle of Wight.

belong to a false man: the false man sees false shows, plausibilities, expediences: the true man is needed to discern even practical truth. Cromwell's advice about the Parliament's Army, early in the contest, How they were to dismiss their city-tapsters, flimsy riotous persons, and choose substantial yeomen, whose heart was in the work, to be soldiers for them: this is advice by a man who *saw*. Fact answers, if you see into Fact. Cromwell's *Ironsides* were the embodiment of this insight of his; men fearing God; and without any other fear. No more conclusively genuine set of fighters ever trod the soil of England, or of any other land.

Neither will we blame greatly that word of Cromwell's to them; which was so blamed: 'If the King should meet me in battle, I would kill the King.' Why not? These words were spoken to men who stood as before a Higher than Kings. They had set more than their own lives on the cast. The Parliament may call it, in official language, a fighting '*for* the King'; but we, for our share, cannot understand that. To us it is no dilettante work, no sleek officiality; it is sheer rough death and earnest. They have brought it to the calling forth of *War*; horrid internecine fight, man grappling with man in fire-eyed rage—the *infernal* element in man called forth, to try it by that! *Do* that therefore; since that is the thing to be done.—The successes of Cromwell seem to me a very natural thing! Since he was not shot in battle, they were an inevitable thing. That such a man, with the eye to see, with the heart to dare, should advance, from post to post, from victory to victory, till the Huntingdon Farmer became, by whatever name you might call him, the acknowledged Strongest Man in England, virtually the King of England, requires no magic to explain it!

Poor Cromwell—great Cromwell! The inarticulate Prophet; Prophet who could not *speak*. Rude, confused, struggling to utter himself, with his savage depth, with his wild sincerity; and he looked so strange, among the elegant Euphemisms, dainty little Falklands, didactic Chillingworths, diplomatic Clarendons! Consider him. An outer hull of chaotic confusion, visions of the Devil, nervous dreams, almost semi-madness; and yet such a clear determinate man's-energy working in the heart of that. A kind of chaotic man. The ray as of pure starlight and fire, working in such an element of boundless hypochondria, *un*formed black of darkness! And yet withal this hypochondria, what was it but the very greatness of the man? The depth and tenderness of his wild affections: the quantity of *sympathy* he had with things—the quantity of insight he would yet get into the heart of things, the mastery he would yet get over things: this was his hypochondria. The man's misery, as man's misery always does, came of his greatness. Samuel Johnson too is that kind of man. Sorrow-stricken, half-distracted; the wide element of mournful *black* enveloping him—wide as the world. It is the character of a prophetic man; a man with his whole soul *seeing*, and struggling to see.

Falklands. Viscount Falkland, one of the Moderates who had joined the king, fell at Newbury, 1643.
Chillingworths. William Chillingworth, a controversialist in favour of toleration.
Clarendons. Earl of Clarendon, royalist historian and statesman.

On this ground, too, I explain to myself Cromwell's reputed confusion of speech. To himself the internal meaning was sun-clear; but the material with which he was to clothe it in utterance was not there. He had *lived* silent; a great unnamed sea of Thought round him all his days; and in his way of life little call to attempt *naming* or uttering that. With his sharp power of vision, resolute power of action, I doubt not he could have learned to write Books withal, and speak fluently enough—he did harder things than writing of Books. This kind of man is precisely he who is fit for doing manfully all things you will set him on doing. Intellect is not speaking and logicizing; it is seeing and ascertaining. Virtue, *Vir-tus*, manhood, *hero*-hood, is not fair-spoken immaculate regularity; it is first of all Courage and the Faculty to *do*. This basis of the matter Cromwell had in him.

One understands moreover how, though he could not speak in Parliament, he might *preach*, rhapsodic preaching; above all, how he might be great in extempore prayer. These are the free outpouring utterances of what is in the heart: method is not required in them; warmth, depth, sincerity are all that is required. Cromwell's habit of prayer is a notable feature of him. All his great enterprises were commenced with prayer. In dark inextricable-looking difficulties, his Officers and he used to assemble, and pray alternately, for hours, for days, till some definite resolution rose among them, some 'door of hope', as they would name it, disclosed itself.

But indeed his actual Speeches, I apprehend, were not nearly so ineloquent, incondite, as they look. We find he was, what all speakers aim to be, an impressive speaker, even in Parliament; one who, from the first, had weight. With that rude passionate voice of his, he was always understood to *mean* something, and men wished to know what. He disregarded eloquence, nay despised and disliked it; spoke always without premeditation of the words he was to use. The Reporters, too, in those days seem to have been singularly candid; and to have given the Printer precisely what they found on their own notepaper. And withal, what a strange proof is it of Cromwell's being the premeditative ever-calculating hypocrite, acting a play before the world, That to the last he took no more charge of his Speeches! How came he not to study his words a little, before flinging them out to the public? If the words were true words, they could be left to shift for themselves.

But with regard to Cromwell's 'lying', we will make one remark. This, I suppose, or something like this, to have been the nature of it. All parties found themselves deceived in him; each party understood him to be meaning *this*, heard him even say so, and behold he turns-out to have been meaning *that*! He was, cry they, the chief of liars. But now, intrinsically, is not all this the inevitable fortune, not of a false man in such times, but simply of a superior man? Such a man must have *reticences* in him. If he walk wearing his heart upon his sleeve for daws to peck at, his journey

Wearing his heart . . . for daws to peck at. Said by Iago of himself in *Othello*, Act I sc. i; meaning that he did not reveal his private thoughts and feelings so that any fool could mock or criticize.

will not extend far! There is no use for any man's
taking-up his abode in a house built of glass. A man
always is to be himself the judge how much of his mind
he will show to other men; even to those he would have
work along with him. There are impertinent inquiries
made: your rule is, to leave the inquirer *un*informed on
that matter; not, if you can help it, *mis*informed; but
precisely as dark as he was! This, could one hit the
right phrase of response, is what the wise and faithful
man would aim to answer in such a case.

Cromwell, no doubt of it, spoke often in the dialect
of small subaltern parties; uttered to them a *part* of
his mind. Each little party thought him all its own.
Hence their rage, one and all, to find him not of their
party, but of his own party! Was it his blame? At
all seasons of his history he must have felt, among
such people, how, if he explained to them the deeper
insight he had, they must either have shuddered aghast
at it, or believing it, their own little compact hypothesis
must have gone wholly to wreck. They could not have
worked in his province any more; nay perhaps they
could not now have worked in their own province. It
is the inevitable position of a great man among small
men. Small men, most active, useful, are to be seen
everywhere, whose whole activity depends on some conviction which to you is palpably a limited one; imperfect,
what we call an *error*. But would it be a kindness
always, is it a duty always or often, to disturb them in
that? Many a man, doing loud work in the world,
stands only on some thin traditionality, conventionality;
to him indubitable, to you incredible: break that beneath

him, he sinks to endless depths! 'I might have my hand
full of truth,' said Fontenelle, 'and open only my little
finger.'

And if this be the fact even in matters of doctrine,
how much more in all departments of practice! He
that cannot withal *keep his mind to himself* cannot
practise any considerable thing whatever. And we call
it 'dissimulation', all this? What would you think of
calling the general of an army a dissembler because he
did not tell every corporal and private soldier, who
pleased to put the question, what his thoughts were
about everything? Cromwell, I should rather say,
managed all this in a manner we must admire for its
perfection. An endless vortex of such questioning 'cor-
porals' rolled confusedly round him through his whole
course; whom he did answer. It must have been as a
great true-seeing man that he managed this too. Not
one proved falsehood, as I said; not one! Of what
man that ever wound himself through such a coil of
things will you say so much?

But in fact there are two errors, widely prevalent,
which pervert to the very basis our judgments formed
about such men as Cromwell; about their 'ambition',
'falsity', and such-like. The first is what I might call
substituting the *goal* of their career for the course and
starting point of it. The vulgar Historian of a Cromwell fancies that he had determined on being Protector
of England, at the time when he was ploughing the

Fontenelle. French advocate, philosopher, and poet (1657–
1757).

marsh lands of Cambridgeshire. His career lay all
mapped-out: a program of the whole drama; which
he then step by step dramatically unfolded, with all
manner of cunning, deceptive dramaturgy, as he went
on—the hollow, scheming 'Υποκριτής, or Play-actor that
he was! This is a radical perversion; all but universal
in such cases. And think for an instant how different
the fact is! How much does one of us foresee of his own
life? Short way ahead of us it is all dim; an *un*wound
skein of possibilities, of apprehensions, attemptabilities,
vague-looming hopes. This Cromwell had *not* his life
lying all in that fashion of Program, which he needed
then, with that unfathomable cunning of his, only to
enact dramatically, scene after scene! Not so. We
see it so; but to him it was in no measure so. What
absurdities would fall-away of themselves, were this
one undeniable fact kept honestly in view by History!
Historians indeed will tell you that they do keep it in
view—but look whether such is practically the fact!
Vulgar History, as in this Cromwell's case, omits it
altogether; even the best kinds of History only remember
it now and then. To remember it duly with rigorous
perfection, as in the fact it *stood*, requires indeed a rare
faculty; rare, nay impossible. A very Shakespeare for
faculty; or more than Shakespeare; who could *enact* a
brother-man's biography, see with the brother-man's
eyes at all points of his course what things *he* saw; in
short, *know* his course and him, as few 'Historians' are
like to do. Half or more of all the thick-plied perver-

'Υποκριτής. 'Hypocrite'; literally 'one who answers', 'an
interpreter'; hence 'play-actor', 'pretender'.

sions which distort our image of Cromwell, will disappear, if we honestly so much as try to represent them so; in sequence, as they *were*; not in the lump, as they are thrown-down before us.

But a second error, which I think the generality commit, refers to this same 'ambition' itself. We exaggerate the ambition of Great Men; we mistake what the nature of it is. Great Men are not ambitious in that sense; he is a small poor man that is ambitious so. Examine the man who lives in misery because he does not shine above other men; who goes about producing himself, pruriently anxious about his gifts and claims; struggling to force everybody, as it were begging everybody for God's sake, to acknowledge him a great man, and set him over the heads of men! Such a creature is among the wretchedest sights seen under this sun. A *great* man? A poor morbid prurient empty man; fitter for the ward of a hospital, than for a throne among men. I advise you to keep out of his way. He cannot walk on quiet paths; unless you will look at him, wonder at him, write paragraphs about him, he cannot live. It is the *emptiness* of the man, not his greatness. Because there is nothing in himself, he hungers and thirsts that you would find something in him. In good truth, I believe no great man, not so much as a genuine man who had health and real substance in him of whatever magnitude, was ever much tormented in this way.

And think now how it actually was with Cromwell. From of old, the sufferings of God's Church, true zealous preachers of the truth flung into dungeons, whipt, set

on pillories, their ears cropt off, God's Gospel-cause
trodden under foot of the unworthy: all this had lain
heavy on his soul. Long years he had looked upon
it, in silence, in prayer; seeing no remedy on Earth;
trusting well that a remedy in Heaven's goodness would
come—that such a course was false, unjust, and could not
last for ever. And now behold the dawn of it; after
twelve years silent waiting, all England stirs itself; there
is to be once more a Parliament, the Right will get a
voice for itself: inexpressible well-grounded hope has
come again into the Earth. Was not such a Parliament
worth being a member of? Cromwell threw down his
ploughs and hastened thither.

He spoke there—rugged bursts of earnestness, of a
self-seen truth, where we get a glimpse of them. He
worked there; he fought and strove, like a strong true
giant of a man, through cannon-tumult and all else—
on and on, till the Cause *triumphed*, its once so formidable enemies all swept from before it, and the dawn of
hope had become clear light of victory and certainty.
That *he* stood there as the strongest soul of England,
the undisputed Hero of all England—what of this? It
was possible that the law of Christ's Gospel could now
establish itself in the world! The Theocracy which
John Knox in his pulpit might dream of as a 'devout
imagination', this practical man, experienced in the
whole chaos of most rough practice, dared to consider
as capable of being *realized*. Those that were highest
in Christ's Church, the devoutest wisest men, were to

Theocracy. Ideal or theory of government in which God is
recognized as the real ruler.

rule the land: in some considerable degree, it might be so and should be so. Was it not *true*, God's truth? And if *true*, was it not then the very thing to do? The strongest practical intellect in England dared to answer, Yes! This I call a noble true purpose; is it not, in its own dialect, the noblest that could enter into the heart of Statesman or man? For a Knox to take it up was something; but for a Cromwell, with his great sound sense and experience of what our world *was*—History, I think, shows it only this once in such a degree. I account it the culminating point of Protestantism; the most heroic phasis that 'Faith in the Bible' was appointed to exhibit here below. Fancy it: that it were made manifest to one of us, how we could make the Right supremely victorious over Wrong, and all that we had longed and prayed for, as the highest good to England and all lands, an attainable fact!

But with regard to Cromwell and his purposes: Hume, and a multitude following him, come upon me here with an admission that Cromwell *was* sincere at first; a sincere 'Fanatic' at first, but gradually became a 'Hypocrite' as things opened round him.

I, for one, will not call the man a Hypocrite! Hypocrite, mummer, the life of him a mere theatricality; empty barren quack, hungry for the shouts of mobs? The man had made obscurity do very well for him till his head was grey; and now he *was*, there as he stood recognized unblamed, the virtual King of England.

Hume. David Hume, Scottish historian and rationalist philosopher 1711-1776.

Cannot a man do without King's Coaches and Cloaks?
Is it such a blessedness to have clerks for ever pestering
you with bundles of papers in red tape? A simple
Diocletian prefers planting of cabbages; a George
Washington, no very immeasurable man, does the like.
One would say, it is what any genuine man could do;
and would do. The instant his real work were out in
the matter of Kingship—away with it!

Precisely here, however, lies the rub for Cromwell.
His other proceedings have all found advocates, and
stand generally justified; but this dismissal of the Rump
Parliament and assumption of the Protectorship, is
what no one can pardon him. He had fairly grown to
be King in England; Chief Man of the victorious party
in England; but it seems he could not do without the
King's Cloak, and sold himself to perdition in order
to get it. Let us see a little how this was.

England, Scotland, Ireland, all lying now subdued
at the feet of the Puritan Parliament, the practical
question arose, What was to be done with it? How
will you govern these Nations, which Providence in a
wondrous way has given-up to your disposal? Clearly
those hundred surviving members of the Long Parliament, who sit there as supreme authority, cannot continue for ever to sit. What *is* to be done? It was a
question which theoretical constitution-builders may find
easy to answer; but to Cromwell, looking there into the

Diocletian. Roman emperor, A.D. 284–313. After abdicating
in the latter year he is said to have spent the rest of his days in
cultivating his garden.

real practical facts of it, there could be none more complicated. He asked of the Parliament, What it was they would decide upon? It was for the Parliament to say. Yet the Soldiers too, however contrary to Formula, they who had purchased this victory with their blood, it seemed to them that they also should have something to say in it! We will not 'For all our fighting have nothing but a little piece of paper'. We understand that the Law of God's Gospel, to which He through us has given the victory, shall establish itself, or try to establish itself, in this land!

For three years, Cromwell says, this question had been sounded in the ears of the Parliament. They could make no answer; nothing but talk, talk. Perhaps it lies in the nature of parliamentary bodies; perhaps no Parliament could in such case make any answer but even that of talk, talk! Nevertheless the question must and shall be answered. You sixty men there, becoming fast odious, even despicable, to the whole nation, whom the nation already calls Rump Parliament, *you* cannot continue to sit there: who or what then is to follow? 'Free Parliament', right of Election, Constitutional Formulas of one sort or the other—the thing is a hungry Fact coming on us, which we must answer or be devoured by it! And who are you that prate of Constitutional Formulas, rights of Parliament? You have had to kill your King, to make Pride's Purges, to expel and banish by the law of the stronger whosoever

Pride's Purges. In 1648 about one hundred and forty members favourable to Charles I were refused admission to Parliament by a military force under Colonel Pride.

G

would not let your Cause prosper: there are but fifty or three-score of you left there, debating in these days. Tell us what we shall do; not in the way of Formula, but of practicable Fact!

Parliaments having failed, there remained nothing but the way of Despotism. Military Dictators, each with his district, to *coerce* the Royalists and other gainsayers, to govern them, if not by act of Parliament, then by the sword. Formula shall *not* carry it, while the Reality is here! I will go on, protecting oppressed Protestants abroad, appointing just judges, wise managers, at home, cherishing true Gospel ministers; doing the best I can to make England a Christian England, greater than old Rome, the Queen of Protestant Christianity; I, since you will not help me; I while God leaves me life! Why did he not give it up; retire into obscurity again, since the Law would not acknowledge him? cry several. That is where they mistake. For him there was no giving of it up! Prime Ministers have governed countries, Pitt, Pombal, Choiseul; and their word was a law while it held: but this Prime Minister was one that *could not get resigned*. Let him once resign, Charles Stuart and the Cavaliers waited to kill him; to kill the Cause *and* him. Once embarked, there is no retreat, no return. This

Pitt. William Pitt, the younger, said to have been regarded by George III as a master rather than a minister.

Pombal. Marquis de Pombal, eighteenth-century Portuguese premier, who ruled by terror; he expelled the Jesuits from Portugal.

Choiseul. Minister of France, 1758–70.

Prime Minister could *retire* nowhither except into his tomb.

One is sorry for Cromwell in his old days. His complaint is incessant of the heavy burden Providence has laid on him. Heavy; which he must bear till death. Old Colonel Hutchinson, as his wife relates it, Hutchinson, his old battle-mate, coming to see him on some indispensable business, much against his will— Cromwell 'follows him to the door', in a most fraternal, domestic, conciliatory style; begs that he would be reconciled to him, his old brother in arms; says how much it grieves him to be misunderstood, deserted by true fellow-soldiers, dear to him from of old: the rigorous Hutchinson, cased in his republican formula, sullenly goes his way. And the man's head now white; his strong arm growing weary with its long work! I think always too of his poor Mother, now very old, living in that Palace of his; a right brave woman: as indeed they lived all an honest God-fearing Household there: if he heard a shot go off, she thought it was her son killed. He had to come to her at least once a day, that she might see with her own eyes that he was yet living. The poor old Mother!——What had this man gained; what had he gained? He had a life of sore strife and toil, to his last day. Fame, ambition, place in History? His dead body was hung in chains; his 'place in History'—place in History forsooth!—has been a place of ignominy, accusation, blackness, and disgrace; and here, this day, who knows if it is not rash in me to be among the first that ever ventured to pronounce him not a knave and a liar, but a genuinely honest man! Peace to him. Did he not, in spite of all, accomplish much for us? *We* walk smoothly over his great rough heroic life; step-over his body sunk in the ditch there. We need not *spurn* it, as we step on it!—Let the Hero rest. It was not to *men's* judgment that he appealed; nor have men judged him very well.

SELF-PORTRAIT

IN our wild Seer, shaggy, unkempt, like a Baptist living on locusts and wild honey, there is an untutored energy, a silent, as it were unconscious, strength, which, except in the higher walks of Literature, must be rare. Many a deep glance, and often with unspeakable precision, has he cast into mysterious Nature, and the still more mysterious Life of Man. Wonderful it is with what cutting words, now and then, he severs asunder the confusion; shears down, were it furlongs deep, into the true centre of the matter; and there not only hits the nail on the head, but with crushing force smites it home, and buries it. On the other hand, let us be free to admit, he is the most unequal writer breathing. Often after some such feat, he will play truant for long pages, and go dawdling and dreaming, and mumbling and maundering the merest commonplaces, as if he were asleep with eyes open, which indeed he is.

Of his boundless Learning, and how all reading and literature in most known tongues, we shall say nothing: for unexampled as it is with us, to the Germans such universality of study passes without wonder, as a thing

Our wild Seer. In *Sartor Resartus* ('The tailor repatched', i.e. the work done over again, and done better) Carlyle's philosophy is expounded through the mouth of an imaginary German professor, Diogenes Teufelsdröckh, who is recognizable as Carlyle himself.

commendable, indeed, but natural, indispensable, and
there of course. A man that devotes his life to learning,
shall he not be learned?

In respect of style our Author manifests the same
genial capability, marred too often by the same rudeness, inequality, and apparent want of intercourse with
the higher classes. Occasionally, as above hinted, we
find consummate vigour, a true inspiration; his burning
thoughts step forth in fit burning words, like so many
full-formed Minervas, issuing amid flame and splendour
from Jove's head; a rich, idiomatic diction, picturesque
allusions, fiery poetic emphasis, or quaint tricksy turns;
all the graces and terrors of a wild Imagination, wedded
to the clearest Intellect, alternate in beautiful vicissitude. Were it not that sheer sleeping and soporific
passages; circumlocutions, repetitions, touches even of
pure doting jargon, so often intervene! On the whole,
Professor Teufelsdröckh is not a cultivated writer. Of
his sentences perhaps not more than nine-tenths stand
straight on their legs; the remainder are in quite angular
attitudes, buttressed-up by props (of parentheses and
dashes), and ever with this or the other tagrag hanging
from them; a few even sprawl-out helplessly on all
sides, quite broken-backed and dismembered. Nevertheless, in almost his very worst moods, there lies in
him a singular attraction. A wild tone pervades the
whole utterance of the man, like its keynote and regu-
ator; now screwing itself aloft as into the Song of
Spirits, or else the shrill mockery of Fiends; now sinking
in cadences, not without melodious heartiness, though
sometimes abrupt enough, into the common pitch,

when we hear it only as a monotonous hum; of which hum the true character is extremely difficult to fix. Up to this hour we have never fully satisfied ourselves whether it is a tone and hum of real Humour, which we reckon among the very highest qualities of genius, or some echo of mere Insanity and Inanity, which doubtless ranks below the very lowest.

Under a like difficulty, in spite even of our personal intercourse, do we still lie with regard to the Professor's moral feeling. Gleams of an ethereal Love burst forth from him, soft wailings of infinite pity; he could clasp the whole Universe into his bosom, and keep it warm; it seems as if under that rude exterior there dwelt a very seraph. Then again he is so sly and still, so imperturbably saturnine; shows such indifference, malign coolness towards all that men strive after; and ever with some half-visible wrinkle of a bitter sardonic humour, if indeed it be not mere stolid callousness— that you look on him almost with a shudder, as on some incarnate Mephistopheles, to whom this great terrestrial and celestial Round, after all, were but some huge foolish Whirligig, where kings and beggars, and angels and demons, and stars and street-sweepings, were chaotically whirled, in which only children could take interest. His look, as we mentioned, is probably the gravest ever seen: yet it is not of that cast-iron gravity frequent enough among our own Chancery suitors; but rather the gravity as of some silent, high-encircled mountain-pool, perhaps the crater of an extinct volcano;

Chancery suitors. Persons awaiting lengthy legal process in settlement of suits in the High Court.

into whose black deeps you fear to gaze: those eyes, those lights that sparkle in it, may indeed be reflexes of the heavenly Stars, but perhaps also glances from the region of Nether Fire!

Certainly a most involved, self-secluded, altogether enigmatic nature, this of Teufelsdröckh! Here, however, we gladly recall to mind that once we saw him *laugh*; once only, perhaps it was the first and last time in his life; but then such a peal of laughter, enough to have awakened the Seven Sleepers! It was of Jean Paul's doing: some single billow in that vast World-Mahlstrom of Humour, with its heaven-kissing coruscations, which is now, alas, all congealed in the frost of death! The large-bodied Poet and the small, both large enough in soul, sat talking miscellaneously together, the present Editor being privileged to listen; and now Paul, in his serious way, was giving one of those inimitable 'Extra-harangues'; and, as it chanced, On the Proposal for a *Cast-metal King*: gradually a light kindled in our Professor's eyes and face, a beaming, mantling, loveliest light; through those murky features, a radiant, ever-young Apollo looked; and he burst forth like the neighing of all Tattersall's—tears streaming down his cheeks, pipe held aloft, foot clutched into the air—loud, long-continuing, uncontrollable; a laugh not of the face and diaphragm only, but of the whole man from head to heel. The present Editor, who laughed indeed, yet with measure, began to fear all was not right: however,

---

Jean Paul. Jean Paul Richter, famous German author and critic (died 1825), whose influence on Carlyle was almost as great as that of Goethe.

Teufelsdröckh composed himself, and sank into his old stillness; on his inscrutable countenance there was, if anything, a slight look of shame; and Richter himself could not rouse him again. Readers who have any tincture of Psychology know how much is to be inferred from this; and that no man who has once heartily and wholly laughed can be altogether irreclaimably bad. How much lies in Laughter: the cipher-key, wherewith we decipher the whole man! Some men wear an everlasting barren simper; in the smile of others lies a cold glitter as of ice: the fewest are able to laugh, what can be called laughing, but only sniff and titter and snigger from the throat outwards; or at best, produce some whiffling husky cachinnation, as if they were laughing through wool: of none such comes good. The man who cannot laugh is not only fit for treasons, stratagems, and spoils; but his whole life is already a treason and a stratagem.

Fit for treasons . . . spoils. Said by Lorenzo (*Merchant of Venice*, Act V sc. i) of 'The man that hath no music in himself'.

HISTORICAL EPISODES

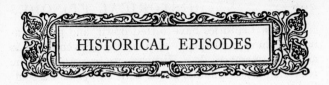

ON HISTORY

By very nature it is a labyrinth and chaos, this that we call Human History; an *abatis* of trees and brushwood, a world-wide jungle, at once growing and dying. Under the green foliage and blossoming fruit-trees of To-day, there lie, rotting slower or faster, the forests of all other Years and Days. Some have rotted fast, plants of annual growth, and are long since quite gone to inorganic mould; others are like the aloe, growths that last a thousand or three thousand years. You will find them in all stages of decay and preservation; down deep to the beginnings of the History of Man. Think where our Alphabetic Letters came from, where our Speech itself came from; the Cookeries we live by, the Masonries we lodge under! You will find fibrous roots of this day's Occurrences among the dust of Cadmus and Trismegistus, of Tubalcain and Triptolemus; the tap-roots of them are with Father Adam himself and the cinders of Eve's first fire! At bottom, there is no perfect History; there is none such conceivable.

Cadmus. Legendary founder of Thebes, said to have introduced letters into Greece.

Trismegistus. Egyptian deity, identified with Hermes.

Tubalcain. First worker in metals (Genesis iv 22).

Triptolemus. Father of agriculture.

All past Centuries have rotted down, and gone confusedly dumb and quiet, even as that Seventeenth is now threatening to do. Histories are *as* perfect as the Historian is wise, and is gifted with an eye and a soul! For the leafy blossoming Present Time springs from the whole Past, remembered and unrememberable, so confusedly as we say—and truly the Art of History, the grand difference between a Dryasdust and a sacred Poet, is very much even this: To distinguish well what does still reach to the surface, and is alive and frondent for us; and what reaches no longer to the surface, but moulders safe underground, never to send forth leaves or fruit for mankind any more: of the former we shall rejoice to hear; to hear of the latter will be an affliction to us; of the latter only Pedants and Dullards, and disastrous *male*factors to the world, will find good to speak. By wise memory and by wise oblivion: it lies all there! Without oblivion, there is no remembrance possible. When both oblivion and memory are wise, when the general soul of man is clear, melodious, true, there may come a modern *Iliad* as memorial of the Past: when both are foolish, and the general soul is overclouded with confusions, with unveracities and discords, there is a 'Rushworthian chaos'. Let Dryasdust be blamed, beaten with stripes if you will; but let it be with pity, with blame to Fate chiefly. Alas, when sacred Priests are arguing about 'black and white surplices'; and sacred Poets have long *professedly*

Rushworthian chaos. John Rushworth was a seventeenth-century Puritan historian, whose massive but chaotic works are typical of the period.

deserted Truth, and gone a woolgathering after 'Ideals'
and such like, what can you expect of poor secular
Pedants? The labyrinth of History must grow ever
darker, more intricate and dismal; vacant cargoes of
'Ideals' will arrive yearly, to be cast into the oven;
and noble Heroisms of Fact, given up to Dryasdust,
will be buried in a very disastrous manner!—

DEATH-WARRANT OF CHARLES I

OLIVER CROMWELL attends in the High Court of Justice at every session except one; Fairfax sits only in the first. Ludlow, Whalley, Walton, names known to us, are also constant attendants in that High Court, during that long-memorable Month of January 1649. The King is thrice brought to the Bar; refuses to plead, comports himself with royal dignity, with royal haughtiness, strong in his divine right; 'smiles' contemptuously, 'looks with an austere countenance'—does not seem, till the very last, to have fairly believed that they would dare to sentence him. But they were men sufficiently provided with daring; men, we are bound to see, who sat there as in the Presence of the Maker of all men, as executing the judgments of Heaven above, and had not the fear of any man or thing on the Earth below. Bradshaw said to the King, 'Sir, you are not permitted to issue out in these discoursings. This Court is satisfied of its authority. No Court will bear to hear its authority questioned, in that manner'.—'Clerk, read the Sentence!'—

And so, under date, Monday 29th January 1648-9, there is this stern Document to be introduced; not specifically of Oliver's composition; but expressing in

Bradshaw. John Bradshaw, president at the trial.

every letter of it the conviction of Oliver's heart, in this, one of his most important appearances on the stage of earthly life.

To Colonel Francis Hacker, Colonel Huncks, and Lieu-tenant-Colonel Phayr, and to every of them.

> At the High Court of Justice for the Trying and Judging of Charles Stuart, King of England, 29th January 1648.

WHEREAS Charles Stuart, King of England, is and standeth convicted, attainted and condemned of High Treason and other high Crimes; and Sentence upon Saturday last was pronounced against him by this Court, To be put to death by the severing of his head from his body; of which Sentence execution yet remaineth to be done:

These are therefore to will and require you to see the said Sentence executed, in the open Street before Whitehall, upon the morrow, being the Thirtieth day of this instant month of January, between the hours of Ten in the morning and Five in the afternoon, with full effect. And for so doing, this shall be your warrant.

And these are to require all Officers and Soldiers, and others the good People of this Nation of England, to be assisting unto you in this service.

Given under our hands and seals,

> JOHN BRADSHAW.
> THOMAS GREY, 'LORD GROBY'.
> OLIVER CROMWELL.
>
> ('and Fifty-six others.')

'*Tetræ belluæ, ac molossis suis ferociores*, Hideous monsters, more ferocious than their own mastiffs!'

shrieks Saumaise; shrieks all the world, in unmelodious soul-confusing diapason of distraction—happily at length grown very faint in our day. The truth is, no modern reader can conceive the then atrocity, ferocity, unspeakability of this fact. First, after long reading in the old dead Pamphlets does one see the magnitude of it. To be equalled, nay to be preferred think some, in point of horror, to 'the Crucifixion of Christ'. Alas, in these irreverent times of ours, if all the Kings of Europe were cut in piéces at one swoop, and flung in heaps in St. Margaret's Churchyard on the same day, the emotion would, in strict arithmetical truth, be small in comparison! We know it not, this atrocity of the English Regicides; shall never know it. I reckon it perhaps the most daring action any Body of Men to be met with in History ever, with clear consciousness, deliberately set themselves to do. Dread Phantoms, glaring supernal on you—when once they are quelled and their light snuffed out, none knows the terror of the Phantom! The Phantom is a poor paper-lantern with a candle-end in it, which any whipster dare now beard.

A certain Queen in some South-Sea Island, I have read in Missionary Books, had been converted to Christianity; did not any longer believe in the old gods. She assembled her people; said to them: 'My faithful People, the gods do *not* dwell in that burning-mountain in the centre of our Isle. That is not God; no, that is

Saumaise. Wrote a defence of the king (*Salmasii Defensio Regia,* printed 1650); answered by Milton.
St. Margaret's Churchyard. At Westminster, near the Houses of Parliament.

a common burning-mountain—mere culinary fire burning under peculiar circumstances. See, I will walk before you to that burning-mountain; will empty my wash-bowl into it, cast my slipper over it, defy it to the uttermost, and stand the consequences!'—She walked accordingly, this South-Sea Heroine, nerved to the sticking-place; her people following in pale horror and expectancy: she did her experiment—and, I am told, they have truer notions of the gods in that Island ever since! Experiment which it is now very easy to *repeat*, and very needless. Honour to the Brave who deliver us from Phantom-dynasties, in South-Sea Islands and in North!

This action of the English Regicides did in effect strike a damp like death through the heart of Flunkeyism universally in this world. Whereof Flunkeyism, Cant, Cloth-worship, or whatever ugly name it have, has gone about incurably sick ever since; and is now at length, in these generations, very rapidly dying. The like of which action will not be needed for a thousand years again. Needed, alas—not till a new genuine Hero-worship has arisen, has perfected itself; and had time to degenerate into a Flunkeyism and Cloth-worship again! Which I take to be a very long date indeed.

THE MASSACRE IN PIEDMONT

JUNE 3rd, 1655. This day come sad news out of
Piedmont; confirmation of bad rumours there had been,
which deeply affects all pious English hearts, and the
Protector's most of all. It appears the Duke of Savoy
had, not long since, decided on having certain poor
Protestant subjects of his converted at last to the
Catholic Religion. Poor Protestant people, who dwell
in the obscure Valleys 'of Lucerna, of Perosa and St.
Martin', among the feeders of the Po, in the Savoy Alps:
they are thought to be descendants of old Waldenses;
a pious inoffensive people; dear to the hearts and
imaginations of all Protestant men. These, it would
appear, the Duke of Savoy, in the past year, undertook
to himself to get converted; for which object he sent
friars to preach among them. The friars could convert
nobody; one of the friars, on the contrary, was found
assassinated—signal to the rest that they had better
take themselves away. The Duke thereupon sent other
missionaries: six regiments of Catholic soldiers; and an
order to the People of the Valleys either to be converted
straightway, or quit the country at once. They could
not be converted all at once: neither could they quit
the country well; the month was December; among the
Alps; and it was their home for immemorial years!
Six regiments, however, say they must; six Catholic
regiments—and three of them are Irish, made of the

banished *Kurisees* we knew long since; whose humour, on such an occasion, we can guess at! It is admitted they behaved 'with little ceremony'; it is not to be denied they behaved with much bluster and violence: ferocities, atrocities, to the conceivable amount, still stand in authentic black-on-white against them. The Protestants of the Valleys were violently driven out of house and home, not without slaughters and tortures by the road—had to seek shelter in French Dauphiné or where they could; and, in mute or spoken supplication, appeal to all generous hearts of men. The saddest confirmation of the actual banishment, the actual violences done, arrives at Whitehall this day, 3rd June 1655.

Pity is perennial: 'Ye have *compassion* on one another'—is it not notable, beautiful? In our days too, there are Polish Balls and such like: but the pity of the Lord Protector and Puritan England for these poor Protestants among the Alps is not to be measured by ours. The Lord Protector is melted into tears, and roused into sacred fire. This day the French Treaty, not unimportant to him, was to be signed: this day he refuses to sign it till the King and Cardinal undertake to assist him in getting right done in those poor Valleys. He sends the poor exiles £2,000 from his own purse; appoints a Day of Humiliation and a general Collection over England for that object—has, in short, decided that he will bring help to these poor men; that England and he will see them helped and righted. How Envoys

Polish Balls. As an example of modern charity.
Ye have compassion. Quoting Mahomet.

were sent; how blind Milton wrote Letters to all Protestant States, calling on them for co-operation; how the French Cardinal was shy to meddle, and yet had to meddle, and compel the Duke of Savoy, much astonished at the business, to do justice and *not* what he liked with his own; all this, recorded in the unreadablest stagnant deluges of old Official Correspondence, is very certain, and ought to be fished therefrom and made more apparent.

In all which, as we can well believe, it was felt that the Lord Protector had been the Captain of England, and had truly expressed the heart and done the will of England—in this, as in some other things. Milton's Sonnet and Six Latin Letters are still readable; the Protector's Act otherwise remains mute hitherto. Small damage to the Protector, if no other suffer thereby! Let it stand here as a symbol to us of his Foreign Policy in general; which had this one object, testified in all manner of negotiations and endeavours, noticed by us and not noticed, To make England Queen of the Protestant world; her, if there were no worthier Queen. To unite the Protestant world of struggling Light against the Papist world of potent Darkness. To stand upon God's Gospel, as the actual intrinsic Fact of this Practical Earth; and defy all potency of Devil's Gospels on the strength of that. Wherein, again, Puritan England felt gradually that this Oliver *was* her Captain; and in heart could not but say, Long life to him; as we do now.

Milton's Sonnet. On the Late Massacre in Piedmont; one of his best-known sonnets. As Latin Secretary to the Council of State he was responsible for the Letters referred to.

DEATH OF CROMWELL

ON Monday, 30th August [1658], there roared and howled all day a mighty storm of wind. Ludlow, coming up to Town from Essex, could not start in the morning for wind; tried it in the afternoon; still could not get along, in his coach, for headwind; had to stop at Epping. On the morrow, Fleetwood came to him in the Protector's name, to ask, What he wanted here?—Nothing of public concerment, only to see my Mother-in-law! answered the solid man. For indeed he did not know that Oliver was dying; that the glorious hour of Disenthralment, and immortal 'liberty' to plunge over precipices with one's self and one's Cause was so nigh! It came; and he took the precipices, like a strong-boned resolute blind gin-horse rejoicing in the breakage of its halter, in a very gallant constitutional manner.

It was on this stormy Monday, while rocking winds, heard in the sickroom and everywhere, were piping aloud, that Thurloe and an Official person entered to inquire, Who, in case of the worst, was to be his Highness's Successor? The Successor is named in a sealed Paper already drawn-up, above a year ago, at Hampton Court; now lying in such and such a place. The Paper

Ludlow. A former member of Council of State.
Fleetwood. Commander of troops in England.
Thurloe. Secretary to Council of State.

was sent for, searched for; it could never be found. Richard's is the name understood to have been written in that Paper: not a good name; but in fact one does not know. In ten years' time, had ten years more been granted, Richard might have become a fitter man; might have been cancelled, if palpably unfit. Or perhaps it was Fleetwood's name—and the Paper, by certain parties, was stolen? None knows. On the Thursday night following, 'and not till then', his Highness is understood to have formally named 'Richard'; or perhaps it might only be some heavy-laden 'Yes, yes!' spoken, out of the thick death-slumbers, in answer to Thurloe's *question* 'Richard?' The thing is a little uncertain. It was, once more, a matter of much moment—giving colour probably to all the subsequent centuries of England, this answer!

On or near the night of the same stormy Monday, 'two or three days before he died', we are to place that Prayer his Highness was heard uttering; which, as taken down by his attendants, exists in many old Notebooks. In the tumult of the winds, the dying Oliver was heard uttering this

PRAYER

Lord, though I am a miserable and wretched creature, I am in covenant with Thee through grace. And I may, I will, come to Thee, for Thy people. Thou hast made me, though very unworthy, a mean instrument to do them some good, and Thee service; and many of them have set too high a value upon me, though others wish and would be glad of my death; Lord, however

Thou do dispose of me, continue and go on to do good for them. Give them consistency of judgment, one heart, and mutual love; and go on to deliver them, and with the work of reformation; and make the Name of Christ glorious in the world. Teach those who look too much on Thy instruments, to depend more upon Thyself. Pardon such a desire to trample upon the dust of a poor worm, for they are Thy People too. And pardon the folly of this short Prayer—Even for Jesus Christ's sake. And give us a good night, if it be Thy pleasure. Amen.

Thursday night the Writer of our old Pamphlet was himself in attendance on his Highness; and has preserved a trait or two; with which let us hasten to conclude. To-morrow is September Third, always kept as a Thanksgiving day, since the Victories of Dunbar and Worcester. The wearied one, 'that very night before the Lord took him to his everlasting rest', was heard thus, with oppressed voice, speaking:

' "Truly God is good; indeed He is; He will not——" Then his speech failed him, but as I apprehended, it was: "He will not leave me." This saying: "God is good", he frequently used all along; and would speak it with much cheerfulness, and fervour of spirit, in the midst of his pains. Again he said: "I would be willing to live to be farther serviceable to God and His people: but my work is done. Yet God will be with His People."

'He was very restless most part of the night, speaking often to himself. And there being something to drink

Writer of our old Pamphlet. Harvey, a Groom of the Bedchamber.

offered him, he was desired To take the same, and endeavour to sleep. Unto which he answered: "It is not my design to drink or sleep; but my design is, to make what haste I can to be gone."

'Afterwards, towards morning, he used divers holy expressions, implying much inward consolation and peace; among the rest he spake some exceeding self-debasing words, *annihilating* and judging himself. And truly it was observed, that a public spirit to God's Cause did breathe in him—as in his lifetime, so now to his very last.'

When the morrow's sun rose, Oliver was speechless; between three and four in the afternoon, he lay dead. Friday, 3rd September 1658.

Oliver is gone; and with him England's Puritanism, laboriously built together by this man, and made a thing far-shining miraculous to its own Century, and memorable to all the Centuries, soon goes. Puritanism, without its King, is *kingless*, anarchic; falls into dislocation, self-collision; staggers, plunges into ever deeper anarchy; King, Defender of the Puritan Faith there can now none be found. . . . The genius of England no longer soars Sunward, world-defiant, like an Eagle through the storms, 'mewing her mighty youth', as John Milton saw her do: the Genius of England, much liker a greedy Ostrich intent on provender and a whole skin mainly, stands with its *other* extremity Sunward;

'*Mewing . . . youth.*' Quoted from Milton's *Areopagitica: A Speech for the Liberty of Unlicensed Printing.* 'Mewing' probably means 'renewing by the process of moulting'.

with its Ostrich-head stuck into the readiest bush, of old Church-tippets, King-cloaks, or what other 'sheltering Fallacy' there may be, and *so* awaits the issue. The issue has been slow; but it is now seen to have been inevitable. No Ostrich, intent on gross terrene provender, and sticking its head into Fallacies, but will be awakened one day—in a terrible *a-posteriori* manner, if not otherwise!——Awake before it comes to that; gods and men bid us awake! The Voices of our Fathers, with thousandfold stern monition to one and all, bid us awake.

THE FRENCH REVOLUTION

I. THE OUTBREAK

THE twelfth July [1789] morning is Sunday: the streets
are all placarded with an enormous-sized *De par le Roi*,
'inviting peaceable citizens to remain within doors', to
feel no alarm, to gather in no crowd.   Why so?   What
mean these 'placards of enormous size'?   Above all,
what means this clatter of military; dragoons, hussars,
rattling in from all points of the compass towards the
Place Louis Quinze; with a staid gravity of face, though
saluted with mere nicknames, hootings, and even
missiles?   Besenval is with them.   Swiss Guards of his
are already in the Champs Elysées, with four pieces of
artillery.

Have the destroyers descended on us, then?   From
the Bridge of Sèvres to utmost Vincennes, from Saint-
Denis to the Champ-de-Mars, we are begirt!   Alarm, of
the vague unknown, is in every heart.   The Palais
Royal has become a place of awestruck interjections,
silent shakings of the head: one can fancy with what
dolorous stound the noon-tide cannon (which the Sun
fires at crossing of his meridian) went off there; bodeful,
like an inarticulate voice of doom.   Are these troops
verily come out 'against Brigands'?   Where are the

De par le Roi. Royal proclamation.
Besenval. Commandant of Paris.

Brigands? What mystery is in the wind? Hark! a human voice reporting articulately the Job's-news: *Necker, People's Minister, Saviour of France, is dismissed.* Impossible; incredible! Treasonous to the public peace! Such a voice ought to be choked in the water-works— had not the news-bringer quickly fled. Nevertheless, friends, make of it what you will, the news is true. Necker is gone. Necker hies northward incessantly, in obedient secrecy, since yesternight. We have a new Ministry: Broglie the War-god; Aristocrat Breteuil; Foulon who said the people might eat grass!

Rumour, therefore, shall arise; in the Palais Royal, and in broad France. Paleness sits on every face; confused tremor and fremescence; waxing into thunder-peals, of Fury stirred on by Fear.

But see Camille Desmoulins, from the Café de Foy, rushing out, sibylline in face; his hair streaming, in each hand a pistol! He springs to a table: the Police satellites are eyeing him; alive they shall not take him, not they alive him alive. This time he speaks without stammering: Friends! shall we die like hunted hares? Like sheep hounded into their pinfold; bleating for mercy, where is no mercy, but only a whetted knife? The hour is come; the supreme hour of Frenchman and Man; when Oppressors are to try conclusions with Oppressed; and the word is, swift Death, or Deliverance

Necker. Appointed Comptroller-General in 1788, was dismissed (or resigned) owing to his financial policy.

Broglie. Duc de Broglie, Marshal of France.

Desmoulins. Advocate of Guise, Picardy; his speech to the Paris crowd marked the beginning of the Revolution.

forever. Let such an hour be *well*-come! Us, meseems, one cry only befits: To Arms! Let universal Paris, universal France, as with the throat of the whirlwind, sound only: To arms—'To arms!' yell responsive the innumerable voices; like one great voice, as of a Demon yelling from the air: for all faces wax fire-eyed, all hearts burn up into madness. In such, or fitter words, does Camille evoke the Elemental Powers, in this great moment. Friends, continues Camille, some rallying-sign! Cockades; green ones—the colour of Hope! As with the flight of locusts, these green tree-leaves; green ribands from the neighbouring shops; all green things are snatched, and made cockades of. Camille descends from his table, 'stifled with embraces, wetted with tears'; has a bit of green riband handed him; sticks it in his hat. And now to Curtius' Image-shop there; to the Boulevards; to the four winds; and rest not till France be on fire!

France, so long shaken and wind-parched, is probably at the right inflammable point. As for poor Curtius, who, one grieves to think, might be but imperfectly paid—he cannot make two words about his Images. The Wax-bust of Necker, the Wax-bust of D'Orléans, helpers of France: these, covered with crape, as in funeral procession, or after the manner of suppliants appealing to Heaven, to Earth, and Tartarus itself, a mixed multitude bears off.

In this manner march they, a mixed, continually increasing multitude; armed with axes, staves, and

D'Orléans. Philippe, Duc d'Orléans, one of the nobility who joined the people's party.

miscellanea; grim, many-sounding, through the streets. Be all Theatres shut; let all dancing, on planked floor, or on the natural greensward, cease! Instead of a Christian Sabbath, and feast of *guinguette* tabernacles, it shall be a Sorcerer's Sabbath; and Paris, gone rabid, dance—with the Fiend for piper!

Raging multitudes surround the Hôtel-de-Ville, crying: Arms! Orders! The Six-and-twenty Town-Councillors, with their long gowns, have ducked under (into the raging chaos)—shall never emerge more. Besenval is painfully wriggling himself out, to the Champ-de-Mars; he must sit there 'in the cruelest uncertainty': courier after courier may dash off for Versailles; but will bring back no answer, can hardly bring himself back. For the roads are all blocked with batteries and pickets, with floods of carriages arrested for examination: such was Broglie's one sole order; the Œil-de-Bœuf, hearing in the distance such mad din, which sounded almost like invasion, will before all things keep its own head whole. A new Ministry, with, as it were, but one foot in the stirrup, cannot take leaps. Mad Paris is abandoned altogether to itself.

What a Paris, when the darkness fell! A European metropolitan City hurled suddenly forth from its old combinations and arrangements; to crash tumultuously together, seeking new. Use and wont will now no longer direct any man; each man, with what of originality he has, must begin thinking; or following those that think. Seven hundred thousand individuals, on the sudden,

Guingette. Roadside inn.

find all their old paths, old ways of acting and deciding, vanish from under their feet. And so there go they, with clangour and terror, they know not as yet whether running, swimming, or flying—headlong into the New Era. With clangour and terror: from above, Broglie the war-god impends, preternatural, with his redhot cannon-balls; and from below, a preternatural Brigand-world menaces with dirk and firebrand: madness rules the hour.

Happily, in place of the submerged Twenty-six, the Electoral Club is gathering; has declared itself a 'Provisional Municipality'. On the morrow it will get Provost Flesselles, with an Echevin or two, to give help in many things. For the present it decrees one most essential thing: that forthwith a 'Parisian Militia' shall be enrolled. Depart, ye heads of Districts, to labour in this great work; while we here, in Permanent Committee, sit alert. Let fencible men, each party in its own range of streets, keep watch and ward, all night. Let Paris court a little fever-sleep; confused by such fever-dreams, of 'violent motions at the Palais Royal' —or from time to time start awake, and look out, palpitating, in its nightcap, at the clash of discordant mutually-unintelligible Patrols; on the gleam of distant Barriers, going up all-too ruddy towards the vault of Night.

On Monday the huge City has awoke, not to its week-day industry: to what a different one! The working man has become a fighting man; has one want only: that of arms. The industry of all crafts has

Echevin. Alderman, or sheriff.

paused—except it be the smith's, fiercely hammering
pikes; and, in a faint degree, the kitchener's, cooking
offhand victuals; for *bouche va toujours*. Women too
are sewing cockades—not now of *green*, which being
D'Artois colour, the Hôtel-de-Ville has had to interfere
in it; but of *red* and *blue*, our old Paris colours: these,
once based on a ground of constitutional *white*, are the
famed TRICOLOUR—which (if Prophecy err not) 'will go
round the world'.

All shops, unless it be the Bakers' and Vintners', are
shut: Paris is in the streets—rushing, foaming like some
Venice wine-glass into which you had dropped poison.
The tocsin, by order, is pealing madly from all steeples.
Arms, ye Elector Municipals; thou Flesselles with thy
Echevins, give us arms! Flesselles gives what he can:
fallacious, perhaps insidious promises of arms from
Charleville; order to seek arms here, order to seek them
there. The new Municipals give what they can; some
three hundred and sixty indifferent firelocks, the
equipment of the City-Watch: 'a man in wooden shoes,
and without coat, directly clutches one of them, and
mounts guard'. Also as hinted, an order to all Smiths
to make pikes with their whole soul.

Heads of Districts are in fervent consultation; subordinate Patriotism roams distracted, ravenous for arms.
Hitherto at the Hôtel-de-Ville was only such modicum
of indifferent firelocks as we have seen. At the so-called
Arsenal, there lies nothing but rust, rubbish, and salt-
petre—overlooked too by the guns of the Bastille. His
Majesty's Repository, what they call *Garde-Meuble*, is

Bouche va toujours. Mouths always need filling.

H

forced and ransacked: tapestries enough, and gauderies; but of serviceable fighting-gear small stock! Two silver-mounted cannons there are; an ancient gift from his Majesty of Siam to Louis Fourteenth: gilt sword of the Good Henri; antique Chivalry arms and armour. These, and such as these, a necessitous Patriotism snatches greedily, for want of better. The Siamese cannons go trundling, on an errand they were not meant for. Among the indifferent firelocks are seen tourney-lances; the princely helm and hauberk glittering amid ill-hatted heads—as in a time when all times and their possessions are suddenly sent jumbling!

At the *Maison de Saint-Lazare*, Lazar-House once, now a Correction-House with Priests, there was no trace of arms; but, on the other hand, corn, plainly to a culpable extent. Out with it, to market; in this scarcity of grains! Heavens, will 'fifty-two carts', in long row, hardly carry it to the *Halle aux Bleds*? Well, truly, ye reverend Fathers, was your pantry filled; fat are your larders; over-generous your wine-bins, ye plotting exasperators of the Poor; traitorous forestallers of bread!

Vain is protesting, entreaty on bare knees: the House of Saint-Lazarus has that in it which comes not out by protesting. Behold, how, from every window, it *vomits*: mere torrents of furniture, of bellowing and hurlyburly —the cellars also leaking wine. Till, as was natural, smoke rose—kindled, some say, by the desperate Saint-Lazaristes themselves, desperate of other riddance; and the Establishment vanished from this world in flame.

Halle aux Bleds. Corn Exchange. *Bleds* is now spelt *Blés.*

Remark nevertheless that 'a thief' (set on or not by Aristocrats), being detected there, is 'instantly hanged'.

Look also at the Châtelet Prison. The Debtors' Prison of La Force is broken from without; and they that sat in bondage to Aristocrats go free: hearing of which the Felons at the Châtelet do likewise 'dig up their pavements', and stand on the offensive; with the best prospects—had not Patriotism, passing that way, 'fired a volley' into the Felon world; and crushed it down again under hatches. Patriotism consorts not with thieving and felony: surely also Punishment, this day, hitches (if she still hitch) after Crime, with frightful shoes-of-swiftness! 'Some score or two' of wretched persons, found prostrate with drink in the cellars of that Saint-Lazare, are indignantly haled to prison; the Jailer has no room; whereupon, other place of security not suggesting itself, it is written, '*on les pendit*, they hanged them.' Brief is the word; not without significance, be it true or untrue!

In such circumstances, the Aristocrat, the unpatriotic rich man is packing-up for departure. But he shall not get departed. A wooden-shod force has seized all Barriers, burnt or not: all that enters, all that seeks to issue, is stopped there, and dragged to the Hôtel-de-Ville: coaches, tumbrils, plate, furniture, 'many meal-sacks', in time even 'flocks and herds' encumber the Place de Grève.

And so it roars, and rages, and brays; drums beating, steeples pealing; criers rushing with hand-bells: 'Oyez, oyez, All men to their Districts to be enrolled!' The

Districts have met in gardens, open squares; are getting marshalled into volunteer troops. No redhot ball has yet fallen from Besenval's Camp; on the contrary, Deserters with their arms are continually dropping in: nay now, joy of joys, at two in the afternoon, the Gardes Françaises, being ordered to Saint-Denis, and flatly declining, have come over in a body! It is a fact worth many. Three thousand six hundred of the best fighting men, with complete accoutrement; with cannoneers even, and cannon! Their officers are left standing alone; could not so much as succeed in 'spiking the guns'. The very Swiss, it may now be hoped, Château-Vieux and the others, will have doubts about fighting.

Our Parisian Militia—which some think it were better to name National Guard—is prospering as heart could wish. It promised to be forty-eight thousand; but will in few hours double and quadruple that number: invincible, if we had only arms!

But see, the promised Charleville Boxes, marked *Artillerie*! Here, then, are arms enough? Conceive the blank face of Patriotism, when it found them filled with rags, foul linen, candle-ends, and bits of wood! Provost of the Merchants, how is this? Neither at the Chartreux Convent, whither we were sent with signed order, is there or ever was there any weapon of war. Nay here, in this Seine Boat, safe under tarpaulings (had not the nose of Patriotism been of the finest), are 'five thousand-weight of gunpowder'; not coming *in*, but surreptitiously going out! What meanest thou, Flesselles? 'Tis a ticklish game, that of 'amusing' us. Cat plays with captive mouse: but mouse with enraged cat, with enraged National Tiger?

Meanwhile, the faster, O ye black-aproned Smiths, smite; with strong arm and willing heart. This man and that, all stroke from head to heel, shall thunder alternating, and ply the great forge-hammer, till stithy reel and ring again; while ever and anon, overhead, booms the alarm-cannon—for the City has now got gunpowder. Pikes are fabricated; fifty thousand of them, in six-and-thirty hours: judge whether the Black-aproned have been idle. Dig trenches, unpave the streets, ye others, assiduous, man and maid; cram the earth in barrel-barricades, at each of them a volunteer sentry; pile the whinstones in window-sills and upper rooms. Have scalding pitch, at least boiling water ready, ye weak old women, to pour it and dash it on Royal-Allemand, with your old skinny arms: your shrill curses along with it will not be wanting! Patrols of the newborn National Guard, bearing torches, scour the streets, all that night; which otherwise are vacant, yet illumined in every window by order. Strange-looking; like some naphtha-lighted City of the Dead, with here and there a flight of perturbed Ghosts.

O poor mortals, how ye make this Earth bitter for each other; this fearful and wonderful Life fearful and horrible; and Satan has his place in all hearts! Such agonies and ragings and wailings ye have, and have had, in all times—to be buried all, in so deep silence; and the salt sea is not swoln with your tears.

Great meanwhile is the moment, when tidings of Freedom reach us; when the long-enthralled soul, from amid its chains and squalid stagnancy, arises, were it still only in blindness and bewilderment, and swears by Him that made it, that it will be *free*! Free? Understand that well, it is the deep commandment, dimmer or clearer, of our whole being, to be *free*. Freedom is the one purport, wisely aimed at, or unwisely, of all man's struggles, toilings, and sufferings, in this Earth. Yes, supreme is such a moment (if thou have known it): first vision as of a flame-girt Sinai, in this our waste Pilgrimage—which thenceforth wants not its pillar of cloud by day, and pillar of fire by night! Something it is even—nay, something considerable, when the chains have grown *corrosive*, poisonous—to be free 'from oppression by our fellow-man'. Forward, ye maddened sons of France; be it towards this destiny or towards that! Around you is but starvation, falsehood, corruption, and the clam of death. Where ye are is no abiding.

Imagination may, imperfectly, figure how Commandant Besenval, in the Champ-de-Mars, has worn out these sorrowful hours. Insurrection raging all round; his men melting away! From Versailles, to the most pressing messages, comes no answer; or once only some vague word of answer which is worse than none. A Council of Officers can decide merely that there is no decision: Colonels inform him, 'weeping', that they do not think their men will fight. Cruel uncertainty is here: war-god Broglie sits yonder, inaccessible in his

Olympus; does not descend terror-clad, does not produce his whiff of grapeshot; sends no orders.

Truly, in the Château of Versailles all seems mystery: in the Town of Versailles, were we there, all is rumour, alarm, and indignation. An august National Assembly sits, to appearance, menaced with death; endeavouring to defy death. It has resolved 'that Necker carries with him the regrets of the Nation'. It has sent solemn Deputation over to the Château, with entreaty to have these troops withdrawn. In vain: his Majesty, with a singular composure, invites us to be busy rather with our own duty, making the Constitution! Foreign Pandours, and suchlike, go pricking and prancing, with a swashbuckler air; with an eye too probably to the *Salle des Menus*—were it not for the 'grim-looking countenances' that crowd all avenues there. Be firm, ye National Senators; the cynosure of a firm, grim-looking people!

The august National Senators determine that there shall, at least, be Permanent Session till this thing end.

So at Versailles. But at Paris, agitated Besenval, before retiring for the night, has stept over to old M. de Sombreuil, of the *Hôtel des Invalides* hard by. M. de Sombreuil has, what is a great secret, some eight-and-twenty thousand stand of muskets deposited in his cellars there; but no trust in the temper of his Invalides.

Whiff of grapeshot. Before the outbreak it was said that the Duc de Broglie, 'with a whiff of grapeshot', would quickly give an account of the mob.

Salle des Menus. Ballroom.

Hôtel des Invalides. Institution for pensioned, disabled soldiers; the Chelsea Hospital of Paris.

This day, for example, he sent twenty of the fellows down to unscrew those muskets; lest Sedition might snatch at them: but scarcely, in six hours, had the twenty unscrewed twenty gun-locks, or dogsheads (*chiens*) of locks—each Invalide his dogshead! If ordered to fire, they would, he imagines, turn their cannon against himself.

Unfortunate old military gentleman, it is your hour, not of glory! Old Marquis de Launay too, of the Bastille, has pulled up his drawbridges long since, 'and retired into his interior'; with sentries walking on his battlements, under the midnight sky, aloft over the glare of illuminated Paris—whom a National Patrol, passing that way, takes the liberty of firing at: 'seven shots towards twelve at night', which do not take effect. This was the 13th day of July 1789; a worse day, many said, than the last 13th was, when only hail fell out of Heaven, not madness rose out of Tophet, ruining worse than crops!

II. THE STORMING OF THE BASTILLE

ALL morning, since nine, there has been a cry everywhere: To the Bastille! Repeated 'deputations of citizens' have been here, passionate for arms; whom De Launay has got dismissed by soft speeches through portholes. Towards noon, Elector Thuriot de la

Marquis de Launay. Governor of the Bastille.
All morning. 14th July 1789.
Elector Thuriot. An Elector Municipal, representative of the citizens.

Rosière gains admittance; finds De Launay indisposed
for surrender; nay disposed for blowing up the place
rather. Thuriot mounts with him to the battlements:
heaps of paving-stones, old iron, and missiles lie piled;
cannon all duly levelled; in every embrasure a cannon
—only drawn back a little! But outwards, behold,
O Thuriot, how the multitude flows on, welling through
every street: tocsin furiously pealing, all drums beating
the *générale*: the Suburb Saint-Antoine rolling hither-
ward wholly, as one man! Such vision (spectral yet
real) thou, O Thuriot, as from thy Mount of Vision,
beholdest in this moment: prophetic of what other
Phantasmagories, and loud-gibbering Spectral Realities,
which thou yet beholdest not, but shalt! '*Que voulez-
vous?*' said De Launay, turning pale at the sight, with
an air of reproach, almost of menace. 'Monsieur,' said
Thuriot, rising into the moral-sublime, 'what mean *you*?
Consider if I could not precipitate *both* of us from this
height'—say only a hundred feet, exclusive of the
walled ditch! Whereupon De Launay fell silent.
Thuriot shows himself from some pinnacle, to comfort
the multitude becoming suspicious, fremescent: then
descends; departs with protest; with warning addressed
also to the Invalides—on whom, however, it produces
but a mixed indistinct impression. The old heads are
none of the clearest; besides, it is said, De Launay has
been profuse of beverages (*prodigua des buissons*).
They think, they will not fire—if not fired on, if they can
help it; but must, on the whole, be ruled considerably
by circumstances.

Wo to thee, De Launay, in such an hour, if thou
    * H

canst not, taking some one firm decision, *rule* circumstances! Soft speeches will not serve; hard grapeshot is questionable; but hovering between the two is *un*questionable. Ever wilder swells the tide of men; their infinite hum waxing ever louder, into imprecations, perhaps into crackle of stray musketry—which latter, on walls nine feet thick, cannot do execution. The Outer Drawbridge has been lowered for Thuriot; new *deputation of citizens* (it is the third, and noisiest of all) penetrates that way into the Outer Court: soft speeches producing no clearance of these, De Launay gives fire; pulls up his Drawbridge. A slight sputter —which has *kindled* the too combustible chaos; made it a roaring fire-chaos! Bursts forth Insurrection, at sight of its own blood (for there were deaths by that sputter of fire), into endless rolling explosion of musketry, distraction, execration — and over head, from the Fortress, let one great gun, with its grapeshot, go booming, to show what we *could* do. The Bastille is besieged!

On, then, all Frenchmen, that have hearts in your bodies! Roar with all your throats, of cartilage and metal, ye Sons of Liberty; stir spasmodically whatsoever of utmost faculty is in you, soul, body, or spirit; for it is the hour! Smite, thou Louis Tournay, cartwright of the Marais, old-soldier of the Regiment Dauphiné; smite at that Outer Drawbridge chain, though the fiery hail whistles round thee! Never, over nave or felloe, did thy axe strike such a stroke. Down with it, man; down with it to Orcus: let the whole

Marais. Market gardens of Paris.   *Nave.* Hub.
Felloe. Outer rim of a wheel.

accursed Edifice sink thither, and Tyranny be swallowed
up forever! Mounted, some say, on the roof of the
guard-room, some 'on bayonet stuck into joints of the
wall', Louis Tournay smites, brave Aubin Bonnemère
(also an old soldier) seconding him: the chain yields,
breaks; the huge Drawbridge slams down, thundering
(*avec fracas*). Glorious: and yet, alas, it is still but the
outworks. The Eight grim Towers, with their Invalide
musketry, their paving-stones, and cannon-mouths, still
soar aloft intact—Ditch yawning impassable, stone-
faced; the inner Drawbridge with its *back* towards us:
the Bastille is still to take!

To describe this Siege of the Bastille (thought to be
one of the most important in History) perhaps transcends
the talent of mortals. Paris wholly has got to the acme
of its frenzy; whirled, all ways, by panic madness. At
every street-barricade, there whirls simmering a minor
whirlpool — strengthening the barricade, since God
knows what is coming; and all minor whirlpools play
distractedly into that grand Fire-Mahlstrom which is
lashing round the Bastille.

Let conflagration rage; of whatsoever is combustible!
Guard-rooms are burnt, Invalides mess-rooms. A distracted 'Peruke-maker with two fiery torches' is for
burning 'the saltpetres of the Arsenal'—had not a
woman run screaming; had not a Patriot, with some
tincture of Natural Philosophy, instantly struck the
wind out of him (butt of musket on pit of stomach),
overturned barrels, and stayed the devouring element.
A young beautiful lady, seized escaping in these Outer

Courts, and thought falsely to be De Launay's daughter, shall be burnt in De Launay's sight; she lies swooned on a paillasse: but again a Patriot, it is brave Aubin Bonnemère the old soldier, dashes in, and rescues her. Straw is burnt; three cartloads of it, hauled thither, go up in white smoke: almost to the choking of Patriotism itself. Smoke as of Tophet; confusion as of Babel; noise as of the Crack of Doom!

How the great Bastille Clock ticks (inaudible) in its Inner Court there, at its ease, hour after hour; as if nothing special, for it or the world, were passing! It tolled One when the firing began; and is now pointing towards Five, and still the firing slakes not. Far down, in their vaults, the seven Prisoners hear muffled din as of earthquakes; their Turnkeys answer vaguely.

What shall De Launay do? One thing only De Launay could have done: what he said he would do. Fancy him sitting, from the first, with lighted taper, within arm's-length of the Powder-Magazine; motionless, like old Roman Senator, or Bronze Lamp-holder; coldly apprising Thuriot, and all men, by a slight motion of his eye, what his resolution was:—Harmless he sat there, while unharmed; but the King's Fortress, meanwhile, could, might, would, or should in nowise be surrendered, save to the King's Messenger.

And yet, withal, he could not do it. Hast thou considered how each man's heart is so tremulously responsive to the hearts of all men; hast thou noted how

Tophet. Originally a place near Jerusalem where idolatrous Jews worshipped fire-gods and sacrificed children; hence, metaphorically, Hell.

omnipotent is the very sound of many men? How their shriek of indignation palsies the strong soul; their howl of contumely withers with unfelt pangs? De Launay could not do it. Distracted, he hovers between two; hopes in the middle of despair; surrenders not his Fortress; declares that he will blow it up, seizes torches to blow it up, and does not blow it. Unhappy old De Launay, it is the death-agony of thy Bastille and thee! Jail, Jailering, and Jailer, all three, such as they may have been, must finish.

For four hours now has the World-Bedlam roared: call it the World-Chimæra, blowing fire! The poor Invalides have sunk under their battlements, or rise only with reversed muskets: they have made a white flag of napkins; go beating the *chamade*, or seeming to beat, for one can hear nothing. The very Swiss at the Portcullis look weary of firing; disheartened in the fire-deluge: a porthole at the drawbridge is opened, as by one that would speak. See Huissier Maillard, the shifty man! On his plank, swinging over the abyss of that stone Ditch; plank resting on parapet, balanced by weight of Patriots—he hovers perilous: such a Dove towards such an Ark! Deftly, thou shifty Usher: one man already fell; and lies smashed, far down there, against the masonry! Usher Maillard falls not: deftly, unerring he walks, with outspread palm. The Swiss holds a paper through his porthole; the shifty Usher snatches it, and returns. Terms of surrender: Pardon, immunity to all! Are they accepted? '*Foi d'officier*, On the word of an officer,' answers half-pay Hulin—or

Chamade. Parley.

half-pay Elie, for men do not agree on it—'they are!'
Sinks the drawbridge—Usher Maillard bolting it when
down; rushes-in the living deluge: the Bastille is fallen!
Victoire !   La Bastille est prise !

. . . . .

O evening sun of July, how, at this hour, thy beams
fall slant on reapers amid peaceful woody fields; on old
women spinning in cottages; on ships far out in the
silent main; on Balls at the Orangerie of Versailles,
where high-rouged Dames of the Palace are even now
dancing with double-jacketed Hussar-Officers—and also
on this roaring Hell-porch of a Hôtel-de-Ville! Babel
Tower, with the confusion of tongues, were not Bedlam
added with the conflagration of thoughts, was no type
of it. One forest of distracted steel bristles, endless, in
front of an Electoral Committee; points itself, in horrid
radii, against this and the other accused breast. It
was the Titans warring with Olympus; and they, scarcely
crediting it, have *conquered*: prodigy of prodigies;
delirious — as it could not but be. Denunciation,
vengeance; blaze of triumph on a dark ground of terror;
all outward, all inward things fallen into one general
wreck of madness!

COMMENTARY

I. THE VICTORIAN PROPHET

The word 'prophet' in its original Greek form was used of one who spoke for the gods, or interpreted their will. As applied to a writer like Carlyle it is meant to suggest that his purpose is to enlighten men's understanding and arouse them from their torpor. He wrote because he felt urged to make known what he believed to be of vital importance to his fellow-men. From childhood he had known adversity, and his work reflects his experience. Without some knowledge of the facts of his life the reader cannot properly appreciate his outlook and teaching. Born in 1795 at Ecclefechan, a small market town in Dumfriesshire, Thomas Carlyle was the eldest of nine children. His father was a hard-working stone-mason, stern and rugged, a man of few words, but of vivid speech when occasion arose. His mother was of a warmer nature, anxious for the well-being of her son, but shared her husband's deep piety, of the Calvinist kind, and his earnest good sense. 'No man of my day,' he wrote in later life, 'or hardly any man, can have better parents.' His character was also influenced by the two voices of Nature, mountain and sea, for the mountains of Galloway and the Solway Firth were both not far from his home.

After a few years at the village school the boy was sent to Annan Grammar School, where he suffered on account of his sensitive nature, though later his fighting instinct gained him respect. Here he formed the habit that he retained throughout life of wide and intensive reading. At fourteen his parents sent him to Edinburgh University, with the object of preparing for the ministry. During his five years there he lived very frugally and worked hard, distinguishing himself in mathematics. Much to the disappointment of his parents he gave up the idea of entering the Kirk, and for some years earned a precarious living as a tutor, as a teacher of mathematics at his old school, and by writing various articles and translations of French scientific works. He often suffered at this time from acute dyspepsia, a disease that tortured him throughout life and was doubtless partly the cause of his more pessimistic moods. After one period of extreme depression, culminating in three weeks' total sleeplessness, he experienced a spiritual illumination comparable to that of St. Paul or Martin Luther, that completely changed his outlook.

This turning-point in his life took place when he was twenty-five. Filled with a new faith, he now looked upon his poverty and sufferings, and indeed the whole material world, as a delusion—'a hag-ridden dream'— in comparison with the true world of the mind and spirit. The aim of his work henceforth was to awaken people to a sense of their spiritual nature and destiny. He read and absorbed the work of German writers, among whom Goethe, Schiller, and Jean Paul Richter exercised a profound and permanent influence on his outlook. His intense love of books and wide reading in foreign as well as English literature, together with the need to express what he felt and thought, led him to adopt writing as a means of livelihood. In 1824 he published his Life of Schiller and translated *Wilhelm Meister*, the novel by Goethe, who saw in Carlyle 'a new moral force, the extent and effects of which it was impossible to predict'. Two years later he married Jane Welsh, a woman of genius whose criticism proved most valuable. They went to live at Craigenputtock —'the dreariest spot in all the British dominions', as he remarked—on the moors between Galloway and Dumfriesshire, where Mrs. Carlyle had a small farm. For six years they lived here almost in poverty. During this time appeared, among many other pieces, the essays on Burns and Johnson, and *Sartor Resartus*, a kind of spiritual autobiography. Carlyle and his wife then removed to London, settling at Cheyne Row, Chelsea, thenceforward their permanent home.

The great work on the French Revolution, 1837, brought Carlyle a measure of fame though not of fortune. He had lent the manuscript of the first volume to his friend, John Stuart Mill, whose servant used it to light the fire. Reluctantly he accepted £100 from Mill, and after six months' heartbreaking labour rewrote the book. To eke out his livelihood he then began lecturing, a task extremely distasteful to him, but one that enabled him to pay off his debts. His most famous lectures were those on Heroes and Hero-Worship, which were published in book form in 1841. In the previous year Mrs. Carlyle was bequeathed a legacy amounting to about £250 a year, that removed finally all fear of poverty. From this time onwards Carlyle concentrated his attention increasingly on social and political questions. *Past and Present* (1843), the *Life and Letters of Cromwell* (1845), and *Frederick the Great* (completed in 1865), and numerous pamphlets and articles all bear witness to his intense interest in these questions. The death of his great friend, John Sterling, inspired him to write a biography unique in its simplicity of style and tenderness of feeling among Carlyle's works. Another and greater sorrow was caused by the death of his wife, in 1866, soon after he had been elected to the Rectorship of his old university. He survived her fifteen years, a revered figure surrounded by friends; he died in 1881 and was buried at Ecclefechan, in accordance with his own wishes.

The basis of Carlyle's teaching was religion, in the sense of an active faith in ultimate goodness rather than any particular creed. Addressing the students of Edinburgh University, he said: 'No nation that did not contemplate this wonderful Universe with an awe-stricken and reverential feeling that there was a great unknown, omnipotent, and all-wise and all-virtuous Being, superintending all men in it and all interests in it—no nation ever came to very much, nor did any man either, who forgot that'. The England of his day seemed to Carlyle altogether irreligious, bent on seeking material wealth and pleasure in place of spiritual good. Conditions of life were largely the result of the Industrial Revolution, which had begun in the later years of the eighteenth century with the inventions of James Watt, Arkwright, and others. The wealth of the country had increased enormously, but was concentrated in relatively few hands, while the labourers and mechanics were reduced to starvation level. A series of bad harvests increased the distress, and mills were closed down in consequence of 'over-production'. Unemployment, poverty, the growth of ugliness where once had been beauty, above all, the soul-destroying mechanical labour, aroused Carlyle's intense indignation. But the democratic ideals of the French Revolution that found expression in the Chartist movement and the Reform Bill of 1832 did not seem to him to touch the root of the

evil. Political reform and liberty merely transferred
the balance of power from the landowners to the industrialists. Still more strongly he condemned the
doctrine of *laissez-faire*, prevalent among employers, by
which it was believed that the conditions of the people
were governed by immutable economic laws which
would in the long run act for their benefit. The ideal
of liberty on which it was professedly based meant in
practice that employers could treat their workers as
they pleased, without interference of the law.

Carlyle has often been compared with Jeremiah, the
prophet of woe and disaster, a destructive rather than a
constructive critic. The chief evils he denounced were
what he called Mammonism and Dilettantism. The
worship of Mammon he imputed to the new ruling class
of industrialists; dilettanti were the idle land-owning
class who clung to their privileges without regard to
their duties. For the latter class he had only contempt, while for the manufacturers he had some respect
in that they worked with a definite object, even though
that object were merely the accumulation of private
profit. Denunciation, however, was by no means Carlyle's principal object. He saw clearly the need for a
spiritual revolution; justice would triumph in the end,
but only as a result of hard thinking and unremitting
labour. His gospel of work is fundamental in his
teaching: 'Nine-tenths of the miseries and vices of
mankind proceed from idleness'. Literature and the
arts are indispensable as aids to right thinking. 'The
true University is a collection of books', he wrote; but
his choice would not be every man's. All his own work
is marked by an intense vitality: earnestness and
strength were to him prime virtues, the attributes of
the true hero.

II. HIS TREATMENT OF CHARACTER

Most of Carlyle's characters are in some degree 'heroic', in the sense that they exhibit the qualities of wisdom and strength that fitted them to become leaders of the rest of mankind. He believed that the spiritual powers that govern human affairs become incarnated in each epoch as a living Hero, whom all lesser men must worship as an expression of the divine idea. In *Heroes and Hero Worship* he considers various types of hero: the hero as Divinity (Odin), as Prophet (Mahomet), as Poet (Dante, Shakespeare), as Priest (Luther, Knox), as Man of Letters (Johnson, Rousseau, Burns), as King (Cromwell, Napoleon). Obviously the characters chosen are of widely different nature and importance. It is strange to find Dr. Johnson, for example, in the same gallery with Odin, or Burns with Napoleon. It is Carlyle's purpose, however, to reveal the essential or spiritual qualities of these personages, to stress the virtues common to all in their several spheres and the limitations that made some less great than others. Among the virtues, absolute sincerity, clear vision or power of seeing aright, strength of intellect, and will to act aright are required in the hero, and these Carlyle illustrates mainly from a man's life-work. He does not give a mass of facts or attempt to analyse and reveal character in its complex fullness. The reader is expected to have some knowledge of the man and his work, and Carlyle makes frequent allusion to biographical facts. These allusions add to the human interest of the essays and should stimulate the reader not already familiar with the facts to seek them out and test Carlyle's interpretations in their light.

The tendency to simplify and generalize his characters, to ignore details in order to emphasize broad features, is more marked in *Heroes* than in Carlyle's other works. Shakespeare, Burns, Johnson, and the rest are not painted as portraits of living human beings, but are rather treated as expressions of the human spirit. At the same time, sufficient concrete detail is given to indicate their earthly nature. In the picture of Abbot Samson there is far more actual detail. Carlyle develops his character in showing the course of his life, the problems he had to face, his relations with other men, and his everyday life. Yet even here the impression made on the reader is that Carlyle is less interested in human personality than in showing the qualities of a good ruler. 'Abstemious, reticent, rigorous,' he was deeply religious in an age of superstition, he governed his monks sternly but justly and without favour: 'a just, clear-hearted man'. The faults attributed to him by others, that he was tyrannous, hard-tempered, unsocial, ungrateful, contentious, are made to appear the unwarranted grumblings of those not fit for promotion or unable to appreciate the blessings of firm rule. At other times his fits of anger, his impatience with his lazy monks and his own difficulties, his scarce-concealed boasting, are so treated as to appear insignificant or even commendable in a 'brave man, strenuously fighting.'

Abbot Samson is treated as the perfect example of a medieval saint who was also a man of action. The scene of his activities is too remote, and the portrait that emerges is too idealized, to make him an altogether convincing character. Indeed, it is only when Carlyle writes of a man whom he has known personally that he succeeds in presenting a character of flesh and blood. And only in the *Life of John Sterling* does he give us a fully revealed human portrait. Here he shows both the failings, albeit with the sympathy of a close friend, and the virtues of Sterling, by the intimate details of his life, his friendships, his conversation, his personal letters, as well as by his more public actions. The book is written in a clear and tranquil style, very different from Carlyle's usual prose, and ranks as one of the best biographies in the language. Its excellence as a whole, however, cannot be appreciated in short extracts.

The portrait of Coleridge, taken from *Sterling*, is complete in itself, and serves to illustrate Carlyle's method of dealing with a contemporary man of letters. He recognizes certain great qualities, and he gives a vivid likeness of Coleridge's figure and features. He describes in detail his incessant stream of talk, that 'flood of utterance' which held his hearers spellbound, including even Carlyle, impatient as he was to gather definite meanings. 'Glorious islets, too, have I seen rise out of that haze'; but the praise only emphasizes by contrast the condemnation: he has been weighed in the prophet's scales and found wanting. We feel that the picture is one-sided. The standard by which he is judged is too abstract for mere mortals; it is more easily applied to the heroes of the past, whose great actions and utterances stand out above their petty human weaknesses.

III. HIS TREATMENT OF HISTORY

As in his interpretation of human character so in his treatment of history, Carlyle seeks the inner meaning and significance of material facts and circumstances. In his view, history is a revelation of the divine purpose in the world, the truth of which can only be ascertained by laborious study of actual recorded facts. But the material of history is a 'labyrinth and chaos', and only the poet or seer can distinguish between what is vital and what is dead. 'Histories are as perfect as the Historian is wise, and is gifted with an eye and a soul.' Since the divine purpose is expressed in the highest degree through great characters, it follows that 'the soul of the world's history is the history of these'. This view is contrary to that which regards history as dependent upon geographical, economic, and other material conditions, and would not be generally endorsed nowadays; but this is not the place to discuss the various theories put forward by different historians. Carlyle's account of the great men in *Heroes and Hero Worship* may, it is true, give some glimpses into world history, but we do not read the book with that object in view. Nor do we read the story of Samson with the object of contemplating the abbot as the shaper of the destinies of his monks. The chief interest and historical value of that story is due to Jocelyn rather than to Carlyle, though the latter's part in translating and revivifying the language of the original must not be under-estimated.

In treating of Cromwell Carlyle shows more fully than elsewhere, except perhaps in *Frederick the Great*, his view of history as biography. The generally accepted opinion in his time was that Cromwell had 'lived a hypocrite and died a traitor'. Carlyle, convinced of his sincerity and reverencing his powers of leadership, spent 'four years of abstruse toil, obscure speculations, futile wrestlings, and misery' in order to vindicate his character. To master the details of his subject he visited and became familiar with the battlefields of the Civil War and other places associated with his hero. The result was a carefully planned series of Cromwell's letters and speeches, together with a running commentary, that remains to this day an indispensable book for the student of the period. The commentary is mainly for the purpose of revealing Cromwell's character. On occasion Carlyle becomes absorbed in the scene of action and gives a dramatic description of events, at once imaginative and realistic. It is in these pictures, and in the careful editing of the letters and speeches, more than in the commentary on Cromwell's deeds, that lies Carlyle's strength as an historian. His weakness lies in his neglect to state and analyse causes and motives, his obvious bias in favour of Cromwell. For example, Cromwell's destruction of a free Commonwealth by the expulsion of the Long Parliament and the establishment of a despotic Protectorate, and his use of the 'mailed fist' in Ireland, are not merely condoned by Carlyle, they receive his heartiest approval.

Cromwell was written after Carlyle had become obsessed with his doctrine of the Hero. His first, and as many consider, his best historical work, the *French Revolution*, appeared in 1837, before that doctrine had taken shape in his mind. Here is no dominant personality: Danton, Marat, Robespierre, Lafayette stand out clearly portrayed, but interest in them is submerged beneath the rapid action, the crowded scenes of violence, the pictures of sordid common life that afford a kind of light relief. There is no more analysis of the wider questions at issue than in the other books; there is, in fact, less definite and constructive criticism. Carlyle could see nothing but evil in the Revolution; the hope was vain, the causes of liberty and equality for which so many lives were lost were not only delusive but disastrous. The nature of the theme, however, gave full scope to his powers of dramatic narration and description: episodes and incidents are depicted with unequalled skill and force, so that the reader feels himself an actual witness, even an actor, of the drama. Throughout, Carlyle's prophetic voice is heard, striving to show the scene of conflict and the universal madness brought on by men's folly and unbelief in their true perspective in relation to eternal laws of truth and justice.

IV. CARLYLE'S STYLE

Carlyle did not write with a fluent pen. He tells us that he spent two weeks in producing 'two clean pages' of the *French Revolution*; and after the great labour was completed, the average critic was repelled by its rugged, abrupt style. Much of the difficulty of his style arises from the urgency with which he feels impelled to utter his thought. What he has to say is to him of far greater consequence than how he says it. He often seems to be thinking aloud, and the process of thinking is not easy. There is rarely any logical sequence of thought carried on from one paragraph to another. Thought seems continually checked by emotion, and the emotional quality often gives the effect of poetry. In calmer moods Carlyle can write clear and harmonious prose, as in the greater part of the story of Abbot Samson; but most often he is striving to hammer out his truths and arouse the reader by the force of vital language.

Mannerisms are frequent even in his best work.

Among these will be noted the following: undue use of capital letters, dashes, inverted commas and italics; of interjections, foreign words and phrases, and elliptical expression, or omission of words normally required in a sentence; and, more serious, lengthy involved sentences marked by inversions and other peculiarities borrowed from the German. It is important to distinguish between Carlyle's mannerisms, which are the direct result of his mode of thinking, and the conscious tricks of style used by some writers for rhetorical effect. The elaborately built-up sentence, with its balanced phrases and clauses, and the artificial use of similes and other figures as adornments of style seemed to him insincere, tending only to obscure the simple and vital truth. Yet his own style is intensely figurative; metaphor and simile instead of being added as ornaments are the very means by which he expresses himself. His most memorable pictures stand out distinctly and with wealth of detail by the cumulation of similes, metaphors, and striking sharp phrases.

Perhaps Carlyle's chief fault, apart from mannerisms, is exaggeration, an over-emphasis that sometimes gives the impression that he feels the need to shout in order to convince himself. Passionate sincerity and zeal for truth give vitality to his style. What gives it a special flavour is a certain characteristic humour, sometimes kindly, sometimes ironical; usually it is not so much the idea as a quality of the language that is humorous.

V. CARLYLE TO-DAY

One of the most commonly debated questions of the day concerns the relative value of democracy and dictatorship. There has been since the Great War a growing dissatisfaction in many countries with popular governments for their apparent failure to cope with world-wide depression. Many of the economic and other crises due to our industrial civilization Carlyle foresaw, and his warnings and teachings have profoundly influenced men who have been seeking and helping to establish a new social order. It is significant that the rise to power of Fascism in Italy was accompanied by many editions of translations from his writings; and since 1926 selections have sold in Germany to the number, it is said, of 300,000 copies. In a recent book on the Nazi revolution in Germany, a Swedish eye-witness has dwelt on the similarities between the German Chancellor Hitler's thought and Carlyle's. Both are democrats in the sense that they identify themselves with the peasants and artisans, and both aim at redistributing wealth so that the workers may have a fuller share in the life of the community; at the same time, 'both are pronounced intellectual aristocrats with a sublime contempt for the weak-willed, easily led flock of sheep, for characterless mediocrity'. Similarly, Professor Grierson in his recent book, *Carlyle and Hitler*, shows how after a period of neglect Carlyle is coming to be regarded as a prophet to-day. He also reminds us that the worship of the Hero, the cult of the Superman, has its true home in Germany. Carlyle's attempt to plant that Teutonic growth in English soil has never succeeded, because of our long tradition of representative government and relative freedom from disruptive conditions.

Whether or no we accept Carlyle's view of the Hero and his function in society is perhaps not of much importance. There are certain fundamental things in his general teaching that have deeper significance for us to-day. He directs our attention to the prime purpose of human effort, its spiritual nature: 'The world is built, not on falseness and jargon, but on truth and reason'. The rights of man are subordinate to the duties of man. He must exert all his energies that truth and justice may be established. The troubles of the world are at the root due to man's self-seeking, his false notion of happiness as a matter of private profit and private pleasure. True happiness can only be achieved, whether for the individual or the State, in a well-regulated community where the ideal of loyal service is followed with courage and sincerity.

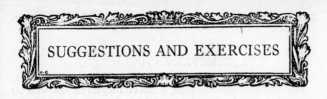

SUGGESTIONS AND EXERCISES

I. ABBOT SAMSON

Books recommended: A. Hamilton Thompson, *English Monasticism* (Cambridge Manuals); Gasquet, *English Monastic Life* and *Greater Abbeys of England* (the former is the standard work on the subject, the latter gives an account of St. Edmund's Monastery); Charles Reade's novel, *The Cloister and the Hearth*.

1. Write an imaginary account of a day in the life of one of Abbot Samson's monks.

2. What is told of Samson before he became abbot? How far is his character already indicated?

3. Compare Abbot Hugo with Abbot Samson.

4. What kings of England are mentioned in the story, and what part do they play in it?

5. Draw up a list of the qualities of Abbot Samson's character, and write a short essay to illustrate them.

6. Describe the election of Samson in the form of a dramatic scene.

7. If you have read anything of Boswell's *Johnson*, explain why Carlyle calls Jocelyn 'a kind of born Boswell'.

8. Summarize the lessons that Carlyle wishes to draw from the story. Add any brief comments you may wish to make.

9. In what respects do you think life in England was happier in Abbot Samson's time than it is now? If you do not think so, give brief reasons.

10. How far does Carlyle reveal his own character in the story?

II. CARLYLE'S CHARACTERS

The student should read a short biography as well as some of the work of each character before reading Carlyle's account. The 'English Men of Letters' Series (Macmillan) for Shakespeare, Burns, Johnson, and Coleridge; Lockhart's *Life of Burns* (Everyman edition), and Frederick Harrison's *Cromwell* (Macmillan) are recommended.

1. In what sense does Carlyle use the word 'Prophet' to describe Shakespeare?

2. Give a list of Carlyle's allusions to actual details of Shakespeare's life and work, and comment briefly on each.

3. Explain the meaning of the following sentence: 'Yet I call Shakespeare greater than Dante, in that he fought truly, and did conquer'.

4. On what grounds does Carlyle consider Burns a Hero?

5. What were, in Carlyle's view, the disadvantages under which Dr. Johnson laboured? How far did they affect his greatness?

6. Make a list of striking phrases by which Carlyle brings out the essential qualities of his characters.

7. Write a short defence of Coleridge against Carlyle's strictures on that poet.

8. Mention some examples to illustrate Carlyle's bias in favour of Cromwell.

9. Which of the characters described by Carlyle appeals to you most? Give a brief account of his life, and point out some characteristics not mentioned by Carlyle.

10. How does Carlyle deal with the charges of hypocrisy, ambition, dishonesty, and intolerance levelled against Cromwell?

III. HISTORICAL EPISODES

A complete edition of *Cromwell's Letters and Speeches* is in 'Everyman's Library', 3 volumes. For the *French Revolution*, the reader should compare Dickens's *A Tale of Two Cities*, a novel which owes much to Carlyle.

1. Compose an eye-witness's account of the execution of Charles I.

2. Write an imaginary dialogue between Cromwell and Charles I, supposed to take place on the day before the execution.

3. Write a short defence either of Charles I or of Cromwell.

4. If you have read *A Tale of Two Cities*, compare Dickens's account of the Fall of the Bastille with Carlyle's.

5. What important personages are described in the *French Revolution*? Show how Carlyle suggests their essential character by the use of brief incisive phrases.

IV. CARLYLE'S LIFE AND TEACHING

Perhaps the most adequate recent account is Louis Cazamian's *Carlyle*, translated by E. K. Brown (Macmillan). Shorter biographies are by John Nichol ('English Men of Letters' Series) and by Richard Garnett ('Great Writers' Series). H. J. C. Grierson's *Carlyle and Hitler* mentioned in the Commentary is published by the Cambridge University Press.

1. What were the chief influences that helped to form Carlyle's character and opinions?

2. Give your own views on Carlyle's doctrine of the Hero and his function in society.

3. Give examples of Carlyle's mannerisms in style. Which do you consider (a) the most irritating, (b) the most pardonable?

4. Write out and memorize a few passages that seem to you especially noteworthy.

5. Write a short essay on the value of Carlyle's teaching to-day.

MADE AT THE
TEMPLE PRESS LETCHWORTH
IN GREAT BRITAIN